LAW AND LITERATURE

Law and Literature

AND OTHER ESSAYS AND ADDRESSES

BY BENJAMIN N. CARDOZO

CHIEF JUDGE OF THE COURT OF APPEALS
OF NEW YORK

Fred B. Rothman & Co.
LITTLETON, COLORADO
1986

Library of Congress Cataloging-in-Publication Data

Cardozo, Benjamin N. (Benjamin Nathan), 1870-1938.
Law and literature and other essays and addresses.

Originally published: New York : Harcourt, Brace, 1931.
1. Law--United States. I. Title.
KF213.C33 1986 349.73 86-6444
ISBN 0-8377-2009-5 347.3

Law and Literature

AND OTHER ESSAYS AND ADDRESSES

BY BENJAMIN N. CARDOZO

CHIEF JUDGE OF THE COURT OF APPEALS
OF NEW YORK

HARCOURT, BRACE AND COMPANY

NEW YORK

Fourth printing, October, 1938

Typography by Robert S. Josephy

PRINTED IN THE UNITED STATES OF AMERICA
BY QUINN & BODEN COMPANY, INC., RAHWAY, N. J.

TO

THE SACRED MEMORY

OF

MY SISTER ELLEN

PREFACE

The essays and addresses brought together in this book may thus be rescued for a while from the oblivion that is the speedy fate of writings, worthy or unworthy, unless durably embalmed.

Some have already been printed in journals, and one as part of a volume in company with the work of others. I offer thanks to the publishers for the privilege of reprinting in this form.

B. N. C.

New York, July, 1930.

CONTENTS

LAW AND LITERATURE

LAW AND LITERATURE[1]

I AM told at times by friends that a judicial opinion has no business to be literature. The idol must be ugly, or he may be taken for a common man. The deliverance that is to be accepted without demur or hesitation must have a certain high austerity which frowns at winning graces. I fancy that not a little of this criticism is founded in misconception of the true significance of literature, or, more accurately perhaps, of literary style. To some a clearer insight has been given. There are those who have perceived that the highest measure of condensation, of short and sharp and imperative directness, a directness that speaks the voice of some external and supreme authority, is consistent, none the less, with supreme literary excellence. A dictum of Henri Beyle's, recalled not long ago by Mr. Strachey, will point my

[1] First published by the Yale University Press in the *Yale Review*, July, 1925.

meaning. The French novelist used to say that "there was only one example of the perfect style, and that was the Code Napoléon; for there alone everything was subordinated to the exact and complete expression of what was to be said." The poor man succumbed to its charm to such an extent that he was in the habit of reading a few paragraphs every morning before breakfast. I do not seek to substitute this regimen for the daily exercise in calisthenics. Some of us prefer our literature like our food in less concentrated tablets. I do no more than suggest that the morsel hastily gulped down may have a savor all its own for the discriminating palate.

But I over-emphasize and exaggerate if I seem to paint the picture of any active opposition that is more than sporadic and exceptional to so amiable a weakness as a love of art and letters. A commoner attitude with lawyers is one, not of active opposition, but of amused or cynical indifference. We are merely wasting our time, so many will inform us, if we bother about form when only substance is important. I suppose this might be true if any one could tell us where substance ends and form begins. Philosophers have been trying for some thousands of years to draw the distinction between substance and mere appearance in the world of matter. I doubt whether they succeed better when they attempt a like distinction in the world of thought. Form is not something added to substance as a mere protuberant adornment. The two are fused into a unity. Not long ago I ran across a paragraph in the letters of Henry James in which he blurts out his impatience of these attempts to divide the indivisible. He is writing to Hugh Walpole, now a novelist of assured position, but then comparatively unknown. "Don't let any one persuade you—there are plenty of ignorant and fatuous duffers to try to do it—that strenuous selection and comparison are not the very essence of art, and that Form *is* not substance to that degree that there is absolutely no substance without it. Form alone *takes*, and holds and preserves substance, saves it from the welter of helpless verbiage that we swim in as in a sea of tasteless tepid pudding." This is my own faith. The argument strongly put is not the same as the argument put feebly any more than the "tasteless tepid pudding" is the same as the pudding served to us in triumph with all the glory of the lambent flame. The strength that is born of form and the feebleness that is born of the lack of form are in truth qualities of the substance. They are the tokens of the thing's identity. They make it what it is.

Up to this point at least, I have little fear of opposition. We shall, most of us, be agreed, I think, not merely that style is not an evil in the Sahara of a judicial opinion, but even that it is a positive good, if only it is the right style. *There* is the disquieting condition which checks the forward movement of triumphal demonstration. What is to be deemed the right style, or the right styles if there are more than one of them? Do the examples of the great masters reveal some uniformity of method for the instruction of the tyro? If uniformity is not discoverable, may there not at least be types or standards? If types or standards do not exist, shall we not find stimulus and interest in the coruscations of genius, however vagrant or irregular? If at times there is neither stimulus nor interest, may there not in lieu of these be the awful warning of example?

I suppose there can be little doubt that in matters of literary style the sovereign virtue for the judge is clearness. Judge Veeder in his interesting and scholarly essay, "A Century of Judicature," quotes the comment of Brougham upon the opinions of Lord Stowell: "If ever the praise of being luminous could be bestowed upon human compositions, it was upon his judgments." How shall his successors in the same or other courts attain that standard or approach it? There is an accuracy that defeats itself by the over-emphasis of details. I often say that one must permit oneself, and that quite advisedly and deliberately, a certain margin of misstatement. Of course, one must take heed that the margin is not exceeded, just as the physician must be cautious in administering the poisonous ingredient which magnified will kill, but in tiny quantities will cure. On the other hand, the sentence may be so overloaded with all its possible qualifications that it will tumble down of its own weight. "To philosophize," says Holmes in one of his opinions—I am quoting him from uncertain and perhaps inaccurate recollection—"to philosophize is to generalize, but to generalize is to omit." The picture cannot be painted if the significant and the insignificant are given equal prominence. One must know how to select. All these generalities are as easy as they are obvious, but, alas! the application is an ordeal to try the souls of men. Write an opinion, and read it a few years later when it is dissected in the briefs of counsel. You will learn for the first time the limitations of the power of speech, or, if not those of speech in general, at all events your own. All sorts of gaps and obstacles and impediments will obtrude themselves before your gaze, as pitilessly manifest as the hazards on a golf course. Sometimes you will know that the fault is truly yours, in which event you can only smite your breast, and pray for deliverance thereafter. Sometimes you will feel that the fault is with counsel who have stupidly misread the obvious, in which event, though you rail against the bar and the imperfect medium of speech, you will be solaced, even in your chagrin, by a sense of injured innocence. Sometimes, though rarely, you will believe that the misreading is less stupid than malicious, in which event you will be wise to keep your feelings to yourself. One marvels sometimes at the ingenuity with which texts the most remote are made to serve the ends of argument or parable. But clearness, though the sovereign quality, is not the only one to be pursued, and even if it were, may be gained through many avenues of approach. The opinion will need persuasive force, or the impressive virtue of sincerity and fire, or the mnemonic power of alliteration and antithesis, or the terseness and tang of the proverb and the maxim. Neglect the help of these allies, and it may never win its way. With traps and obstacles and hazards confronting us on every hand, only blindness or indifference will fail to turn in all humility, for guidance or for warning, to the study of examples.

Classification must be provisional, for forms run

into one another. As I search the archives of my memory, I seem to discern six types or methods which divide themselves from one another with measurable distinctness. There is the type magisterial or imperative; the type laconic or sententious; the type conversational or homely; the type refined or artificial, smelling of the lamp, verging at times upon preciosity or euphuism; the type demonstrative or persuasive; and finally the type tonsorial or agglutinative, so called from the shears and the pastepot which are its implements and emblem.

I place first in order, for it is first in dignity and power, the type magisterial or imperative. It eschews ornament. It is meager in illustration and analogy. If it argues, it does so with the downward rush and overwhelming conviction of the syllogism, seldom with tentative gropings towards the inductive apprehension of a truth imperfectly discerned. We hear the voice of the law speaking by its consecrated ministers with the calmness and assurance that are born of a sense of mastery and power. Thus Marshall seemed to judge, and a hush falls upon us even now as we listen to his words. Those organ tones of his were meant to fill cathedrals or the most exalted of tribunals. The judicial department, he tells us, "has no will in any case. . . . Judicial power is never exercised for the purpose of giving effect to the will of the judge; always for the purpose of giving effect to the will of the legislature; or in other words, to the will of the law." The thrill is irresistible. We feel the mystery and the awe of inspired revelation. His greatest judgments are framed upon this plane of exaltation and aloofness. The movement from premise to conclusion is put before the observer as something more impersonal than the working of the individual mind. It is the inevitable progress of an inexorable force. Professor Corwin in an interesting volume, *John Marshall and the Constitution*, shows how even his contemporaries, the bitterest critics of his aggrandizement of federal power, were touched by this illusion. "All wrong, all wrong," lamented John Randolph of Roanoke, "but no man in the United States can tell why or wherein." I have reread a few of the most famous of his judgments: Marbury *vs.* Madison; Gibbons *vs.* Ogden; McCulloch *vs.* Maryland; they are all in the grand style.

Listen to the voice of the magistrate in Marbury *vs.* Madison: "The distinction between a government with limited and unlimited powers is abolished if those limits do not confine the persons on which they are imposed, and if acts prohibited and acts allowed are of equal obligation. It is a proposition too plain to be contested: that the Constitution controls any legislative act repugnant to it; or that the legislature may alter the Constitution by an ordinary act. Between these alternatives there is no middle ground. . . . If two laws conflict with each other, the courts must decide on the operation of each. So if a law be in opposition to the Constitution; if both the law and the Constitution apply to a particular case, so that the court must either decide that case conformably to the law, disregarding the Constitution, or conformably to the Constitution, disregarding the law, the court must determine which of these conflicting rules governs the case. This is of the very essence of judicial duty." Nothing is here of doubt; nothing of apology; no blurred edges or uncertain lines. "There is no middle ground." The choice that is made is "of the very essence of judicial duty." The voice has pealed forth. Let the wicked heed it and obey.

One will find this same suggestion of sure and calm conviction in some of the judgments of Lord Mansfield. The slave Somerset captured on the coast of Africa, is sold in bondage in Virginia, and brought to England by his master. The case comes before Mansfield on the return to the writ of habeas corpus: "The state of slavery is of such a nature that it is incapable of being introduced on any reasons, moral or political, but only positive law, which preserved its force long after the reasons, occasions, and time itself from whence it was created, are erased from memory. It is so odious that nothing can be suffered to support it, but positive law. . . . I care not for the supposed *dicta* of judges, however eminent, if they be contrary to all principle. The *dicta* cited were probably misunderstood, and at all events they are to be disregarded. Villainage, when it did exist in this country, differed in many particulars from West India slavery. The lord never could have thrown his villain, whether *regardant* or *in gross*, into chains, sent him to the West Indies, and sold him there to work in a mine or in a cane field. At any rate villainage has ceased in England, and it cannot be revived. The air of England has long been too pure for a slave, and every man is free who breathes it. Every man who comes into England is entitled to the protection of English law, whatever oppression he may heretofore have suffered, and whatever may be the color of his skin. '*Quamvis ille niger, quamvis tu candidus esses.*' Let the negro be discharged."

It is thus men speak when they are conscious of their power. One does not need to justify oneself if one is the mouthpiece of divinity. The style will fit the mood.

I have said that in dignity and power there is no method that can be matched with the method which I have characterized as magisterial or imperative. A changing philosophy of law has tended, none the less, to the use of other methods more conciliatory and modest. The development of law is conceived of, more and more, as a process of adaptation and adjustment. The pronouncements of its ministers are timid and tentative approximations, to be judged through their workings, by some pragmatic test of truth. I find in a dissenting opinion by Mr. Justice Brandeis a striking statement of this attitude of mind. Arguing for the restriction of a rule which had proved itself unworkable, he says: "Such limitations of principles previously announced and such express disapproval of *dicta* are often necessary. It is an unavoidable incident of the search by courts of last resort for the true rule. The process of inclusion and exclusion, so often applied in developing a rule, cannot end with its first enunciation. The rule as announced must be deemed tentative. For the many and varying facts to which it will be applied cannot be foreseen. Modification implies growth. It is the life of the law."

One cannot face the law in this spirit of cautious seeking without showing the changing point of view in a changing style and form. Universals will be handled more charily under the dominance of such a philosophy than in days when the law of nature supplied us with data that were supposed to be eternal and unyielding. Yet there are times even now when the magisterial method is utilized by men who know that they are masters of their calling. It is still utilized in fields where some established principle is to be applied to new facts or where the area of its extension or restriction is fairly obvious or narrow. But alas! even then it is the masters, and no others, who feel sure enough of themselves to omit the intermediate steps and stages, and leap to the conclusion. Most of us are so uncertain of our strength, so beset with doubts and difficulties, that we feel oppressed with the need of justifying every holding by analogies and precedents and an exposure of the reasons. The masters are content to say, "The elect will understand, there is no need to write for others." Perhaps there are opinions by Mr. Justice Holmes in which this mood can be discerned. The sluggard unable to keep pace with the swiftness of his thought will say that he is hard to follow. If that is so, it is only for the reason that he is walking with a giant's stride. But giants, after all, are not met at every turn, and for most of us, even if we are not pygmies, the gait of ordinary men is the safer manner of advance. We grope and feel our way. What we hand down in our judgments is an hypothesis. It is no longer a divine command.

I pass to other types which run into each other by imperceptible gradations, the laconic or sententious and the conversational or homely. There has been no stage of our legal history in which these methods have been neglected. The Year Books are full of wise saws and homely illustrations, the epigram, the quip, the jest. Perhaps this is but a phase of that use of the maxim or the proverb which is characteristic of legal systems in early stages of development. Dean Pound in a recent paper has traced the growth and function of the maxim with all the resources of his learning. If the maxim has declined in prevalence and importance, now that the truths of the law have become too complex to be forced within a sentence, there has been no abatement of recourse to the laconic or sententious phrase, to drive home and imbed what might otherwise be lost or scattered. Who will resist Lord Nottingham's adjuration: "Pray let us so resolve cases here, that they may stand with the reason of mankind when they are debated abroad"? Is there any armor proof against a thrust like the dictum of Lord Bowen's: "The state of a man's mind is as much a fact as the state of his digestion"? Next door to the epigram is the homely illustration which makes its way and sinks deep by its appeal to everyday experience. In the wielding of these weapons, the English judges have been masters. The precept may be doubtful in the beginning. How impossible to fight against it when the judge brings it down to earth and makes it walk the ground, the brother of some dictate of decency or of prudence which we have followed all our lives. Perhaps the kinship is not so close or apparent as it is figured. Who of us will have the hardihood to doubt the reality of the tie when it is so blandly assumed to be obvious to all? The common denominator silences and satisfies. The rule that is rooted in identities or analogies of customary belief and practice is felt and rightly felt to be rooted in reality. We glide into acquiescence when negation seems to question our kinship with the crowd. Something must be set down also to the sense of fellowship awakened when judges talk in ways that seem to make us partners in the deliberative process. "I entirely agree with my right honorable and learned friend upon the woolsack." We seem to be let into the mysteries of the conference, the sacrosanct "arcana," to quote Professor Powell's phrase, to which "the uninitiated are not admitted." Given such an atmosphere, with point and pungency thrown into it, the product makes its way into every crack and crevice of our being.

I limit my illustrations, though many are available. Take this by Lord Bramwell: "It does not follow that if a man dies in a fit in a railway carriage, there is a *prima facie* case for his widow and children, nor that if he has a glass in his pocket and sits on it and hurts himself, there is something which calls for an answer or explanation from the company." Take this by Lord Blackburn: "If with intent to lead the plaintiff to act upon it, they put forth a statement which they know may bear two meanings, one of which is false to their knowledge, and thereby the plaintiff, putting that meaning upon it, is misled, I do not think they can escape by saying he ought to have put the other. If they palter with him, in a double sense, it may be that they lie like truth, but I think they lie, and it is a fraud." One could cite other examples without number. What a cobweb of fine-spun casuistry is dissipated in a breath by the simple statement of Lord Esher in *Ex parte* Simonds, that the court will not suffer its own officer "to do a shabby thing." If the word shabby had been left out, and unworthy or dishonorable substituted, I suppose the sense would have been much the same. But what a drop in emotional value would have followed. As it is, we feel the tingle of the hot blood of resentment mounting to our cheeks. For quotable good things, for pregnant aphorisms, for touchstones of ready application, the opinions of the English judges are a mine of instruction and a treasury of joy.

Such qualities on the whole are rarer close at home, yet we have one judge even now who can vie with the best of his English brethren, past as well as present, in the art of packing within a sentence the phosphorescence of a page. If I begin to quote from the opinions of Mr. Justice Holmes, I hardly know where I shall end, yet fealty to a master makes me reluctant to hold back. The sheaf will be a tiny one, made up haphazard, the barest sample of the riches which the gleaner may gather where he will. Some hint of the epigrammatic quality of his style may be found in this: "The Fourteenth Amendment, itself a historical product, did not destroy history for the States and substitute mechanical compartments of law all exactly alike." In this: "We are in danger of forgetting that a strong public desire to improve the public condition is not enough to warrant achieving the desire by a shorter cut than the constitutional way of paying for the change." In this:

"Legal obligations that exist but cannot be enforced are ghosts that are seen in the law but that are elusive to the grasp." And finally in this, words of solemn dissent, their impressiveness heightened by the knowledge that the cause has been already lost: "Persecution for the expression of opinions seems to me perfectly logical. If you have no doubt of your premises or your power and want a certain result with all your heart you naturally express your wishes in law and sweep away all opposition. To allow opposition by speech seems to indicate that you think the speech impotent, as when a man says that he has squared the circle, or that you do not care whole-heartedly for the result, or that you doubt either your power or your premises. But when men have realized that time has upset many fighting faiths, they may come to believe even more than they believe the very foundations of their own conduct that the ultimate good desired is better reached by free trade in ideas—that the best test of truth is the power of the thought to get itself accepted in the competition of the market, and that truth is the only ground upon which their wishes safely can be carried out. That at any rate is the theory of our Constitution. It is an experiment, as all life is an experiment. Every year if not every day we have to wager our salvation upon some prophecy based upon imperfect knowledge. While that experiment is part of our system I think that we should be eternally vigilant against attempts to check the expression of opinions that we loathe and believe to be fraught with death, unless they so imminently threaten immediate interference with the lawful and pressing purposes of the law that an immediate check is required to save the country."

There is another type or method which I have spoken of as the refined or artificial, smelling a little of the lamp. With its merits it has its dangers, for unless well kept in hand, it verges at times upon preciosity and euphuism. Held in due restraint, it lends itself admirably to cases where there is need of delicate precision. I find no better organon where the subject matter of discussion is the construction of a will with all the filigree of tentacles, the shades and nuances of differences, the slender and fragile tracery that must be preserved unmutilated and distinct. Judge Finch of the Court of Appeals of New York was an adept in the writing of opinions which carried with them this suggestion of precision and refinement. Occasionally, it shades into a faint and gentle sarcasm which is sometimes the refuge of the spokesman of a minority expressing his dissent. As an illustration, let me quote from the dissenting opinion in an election controversy which provoked in its day no little warmth of difference. The majority had held that despite the provision of the Constitution making each house of the legislature the judge of the elections, returns, and qualifications of its own members, the courts would refuse affirmative aid to a claimant for such an office if it found him ineligible in its own view of the law. Judge Finch protested against this holding. "And so," he said, "I deny the asserted doctrine of 'Invocation'; of a right to do evil that good may come; of excusable judicial usurpation; and if the doctrine has anywhere got its dangerous and destructive hold upon our law, which I do not believe, it should be resolutely shaken off. But let us not deceive ourselves. The excess of jurisdiction is not even excusable, for it has neither occasion nor necessity." A moment later, he has his fears that he has been betrayed into excessive warmth. His closing words are those of apology and deference: "If what I have said does not convince the majority of the court, nothing that I can say will do so. I have tried faithfully, and, I hope, with proper respect, for certainly I have not meant to be wanting in that, to point out the mistake which, it seems to me, they are about to make. Theirs, however, must be both the responsibility and its consequences."

Such a method has its charm and its attraction, though one feels at times the yearning for another more robust and virile. It is here that I pass into the type which I have characterized as demonstrative or persuasive. It is not unlike the magisterial or imperative, yet it differs in a certain amplitude of development, a freer use of the resources of illustration and analogy and history and precedent, in brief, a tone more suggestive of the scientific seeker for the truth and less reminiscent of the priestess on the tripod. One might cite many judges who have used this method with distinction. I think the work of Charles Andrews, for many years a judge and then the Chief Judge of the New York Court of Appeals, is a shining illustration. I can best describe the quality of his opinions in the words of a memorial written upon his death: "The majesty of his personal appearance," it was said, "is reflected in the majesty of his judicial style, the steady and stately march of his opinions from established premises to inevitable conclusions." Such a method, well pursued, has a sanity and a clarity that make it an admirable medium for the declaration of considered judgments. The form is no mere epidermis. It is the very bone and tissue.

My summary of styles may leave a cheerless impression of the solemn and the ponderous. Flashes of humor are not unknown, yet the form of opinion which aims at humor from beginning to end is a perilous adventure, which can be justified only by success, and even then is likely to find its critics almost as many as its eulogists. The story is told by Bernard Shaw of a man who wished to consult the writings of the great naturalist Buffon, and who startled the clerks in the bookstore by the pompous and solemn query, "Have you the books of the celebrated Buffoon?" One of the difficulties about the humorous opinion is exposure to the risk of passing from the class of Buffons where we all like to dwell and entering the class of the celebrated Buffoons. The transition at times is distressingly swift, and when once one has entered the new class, it is difficult, if not indeed impossible, to climb over the fences and back into the old. None the less, there are subjects which only the most resolute have been able to discuss without yielding to the temptation of making profert of their sense of humor. A dog or a cat, or a horse if it is the occasion of a horse trade, has been the signal for unexpected outbursts of mirth and occasionally of pathos from judges slowly stirred to emotion by the cinema of life.

Judge Allen's opinion on the "code duello"

among dogs, was on the whole a fine success, but it has been responsible for the writing of some others that were not. There is an opinion by Baron Bramwell which deals with the propensities of pigs. A fence was defective, and the pigs straying did mischief to a trolley car. The decision was that the barrier should have been sufficient to protect the adjoining owner against the incursions, not of all pigs, but of pigs of "average vigour and obstinacy." "Nor do we lay down," said the learned Baron, "that there must be a fence so close and strong that no pig could push through it, or so high that no horse or bullock could leap it. One could scarcely tell the limits of such a requirement, for the strength of swine is such that they would break through almost any fence, if there were a sufficient inducement on the other side. But the company are bound to put up such a fence that a pig not of a peculiarly wandering disposition, nor under any excessive temptation, will not get through it." Perhaps the humor of this ruling was more unwitting than designed. Some may agree with Sir Frederick Pollock that the decision is "almost a caricature of the general idea of the 'reasonable man.' " In all this I would not convey the thought that an opinion is the worse for being lightened by a smile. I am merely preaching caution. Other flights and digressions I find yet more doubtful than the humorous. In days not far remote, judges were not unwilling to embellish their deliverances with quotations from the poets. I shall observe towards such a practice the tone of decent civility that is due to those departed.

I have had in mind in this excursus a humor that was conscious and intended. Perhaps I should have classed the opinion that is humorous or playful as an independent type, but I have preferred to treat it incidentally since I am not aware that any judge has employed it consistently or except on rare occasions. Humor also that is unconscious and unintended may be dug out of the reports if we take the trouble to extract it. I once gathered together for my own edification and amusement some gems that I had unearthed from the opinions of one of our local courts in days when it had an appellate branch of its own and handed down opinions which were faithfully reported. Unluckily, I have lost my memorandum, but a few of the items are still vivid in my mind. The question to be determined was the extent of the amendment of a pleading to be permitted upon the trial. The decisive principle was thus expounded: "The bed that litigants make and lie in up to the trial, should not be then vacated by them. They should continue to lie therein until the jury render their verdict." I understand that the modern Practice Acts have swept this principle away, and that the suitor, who seems to his adversary to be innocently somnolent, may now jump out of bed at the last moment and prove to be very much awake. This is the new doctrine, but where will you find a more vivid statement of the doctrine of an elder day which decried surprise and haste, and was satisfied that justice herself should have the privilege of a nap? I recall, too, a charge to a jury, never reported, but surely fit to be preserved. "In this case," said the trial judge, "I believe that Mr. A (the counsel for the plaintiff) knows as much law as Mr. B (the counsel for the defendant), and I believe that Mr. B knows as much law as Mr. A, but I believe that I in my judicial capacity know as much law as both of them together." Whereupon he forgot to tell the jury anything else, but said they were to consider of their verdict and decide the case in accordance with the rules he had laid down. Well, his charge was sparse, but it enunciated an important truth. Our whole judicial system is built upon some such assumption as the learned judge put forward a trifle crassly and obscurely. This is the great convention, the great fiction, which makes trial in court a fair substitute for trial by battle or by casting lots. The philosopher will find philosophy if he has an eye for it even in a "crowner's" court.

I must not forget my final type of judicial style, the tonsorial or agglutinative. I will not expatiate upon its horrors. They are known but too well. The dreary succession of quotations closes with a brief paragraph expressing a firm conviction that judgment for plaintiff or for defendant, as the case may be, follows as an inevitable conclusion. The writer having delivered himself of this expression of a perfect faith, commits the product of his hand to the files of the court and the judgment of the ages with all the pride of authorship. I am happy to be able to report that this type is slowly but steadily disappearing. As contrasted with its arid wastes, I prefer the sunny, though rather cramped and narrow, pinnacle of a type once much in vogue: "We have carefully examined the record and find no error therein; *therefore* the judgment must be affirmed with costs." How nice a sense of proportion, of the relation between cause and effect, is involved in the use of the illative conjunction "therefore," with its suggestion that other minds less sensitively attuned might have drawn a different conclusion from the same indisputable premises.

I have touched lightly, almost not at all, upon something more important than mere felicities of turn or phrase. Above and beyond all these are what we may term the architectonics of opinions. The groupings of fact and argument and illustration so as to produce a cumulative and mass effect; these, after all, are the things that count above all others. I should despair, however, of any successful analysis of problems at once so large and so difficult within the limits of this paper. One needs a larger easel if one is to follow such a map. Often clarity is gained by a brief and almost sententious statement at the outset of the problem to be attacked. Then may come a fuller statement of the facts, rigidly pared down, however, in almost every case, to those that are truly essential as opposed to those that are decorative and adventitious. If these are presented with due proportion and selection, our conclusion ought to follow so naturally and inevitably as almost to prove itself. Whether it succeeds in doing this or not is something about which the readers of the opinion are not always in accord. To gain a proper breadth of view, one should consult counsel for the vanquished as well as counsel for the victor.

The thought of the vanquished brings me to the opinion that voices a dissent. The protests and the warnings of minorities overborne in the fight have their interest and significance for the student, not only of law itself, but of the literary forms through which law reaches its expression. Comparatively speaking at least, the dissenter is irresponsible. The spokesman of the court is cautious, timid, fearful of the vivid word, the heightened phrase. He dreams of an unworthy brood of scions, the spawn of careless *dicta*, disowned by the *ratio decidendi*, to which all legitimate offspring must be able to trace their lineage. The result is to cramp and paralyze. One fears to say anything when the peril of misunderstanding puts a warning finger to the lips. Not so, however, the dissenter. He has laid aside the rôle of the hierophant, which he will be only too glad to resume when the chances of war make him again the spokesman of the majority. For the moment, he is the gladiator making a last stand against the lions. The poor man must be forgiven a freedom of expression, tinged at rare moments with a touch of bitterness, which magnanimity as well as caution would reject for one triumphant.

A French judge, M. Ransson, a member of the Tribunal of the Seine, wrote some twenty years ago an essay on the art of judging, in which he depicts the feelings of a judge of the first instance when a judgment is reversed. I suppose the state of mind of one reversed is akin in quality to the state of mind of one dissenting, though perhaps differing in degree. "A true magistrate," says M. Ransson, "guided solely by his duty and his conscience, his learning and his reason, hears philosophically and without bitterness that his judgment has not been sustained; he knows that the higher court is there to this end, and that better informed beyond doubt, it has believed itself bound to modify his decision. Ought we even to condemn him, if having done his best, he maintains in his inmost soul the impression that perhaps and in spite of everything he was right? *Causa diis victrix placuit, sed victa Catoni.*" Cato had a fine soul, but history does not record that he feared to speak his mind, and judges when in the minority are tempted to imitate his candor. We need not be surprised, therefore, to find in dissent a certain looseness of texture and depth of color rarely found in the *per curiam.* Sometimes, as I have said, there is just a suspicion of acerbity, but this, after all, is rare. More truly characteristic of dissent is a dignity, an elevation, of mood and thought and phrase. Deep conviction and warm feeling are saying their last say with knowledge that the cause is lost. The voice of the majority may be that of force triumphant, content with the plaudits of the hour, and recking little of the morrow. The dissenter speaks to the future, and his voice is pitched to a key that will carry through the years. Read some of the great dissents, the opinion, for example, of Judge Curtis in Dred Scott *vs.* Sandford, and feel after the cooling time of the better part of a century the glow and fire of a faith that was content to bide its hour. The prophet and the martyr do not see the hooting throng. Their eyes are fixed on the eternities.

I shall be traveling away from my subject if I leave the writing of opinions and turn to arguments at the bar. A word of digression may be pardoned, however, for the two subjects are allied. One is called upon often to make answer to the question, what sort of argument is most effective in an appellate court? Shall it be long or short, terse or discursive? Shall it assume that the judges know the rudiments of law, or shall it attempt in a brief hour to supply the defects in their early training? Shall it state the law or the facts? Shall it take up the authorities and analyze them, or shall it content itself with conclusions and leave analysis for the study? There is, of course, no formula that will fit all situations in appellate courts or elsewhere. If, however, I had to prepare a list of "Don'ts" for the guidance of the novice, I think I would say that only in the rarest instances is it wise to take up one decision after another for the purpose of dissection. Such autopsies have their value at times, but they are wearisome and gruesome scenes. In my list of Don'ts, I would add, don't state the minutiae of the evidence. The judges won't follow you, and if they followed, would forget. Don't attempt to supplement the defects of early training. Your auditors are hardened sinners, not easily redeemed. Above all, don't be long-winded. I have in mind a lawyer, now lifted to the bench, who argued the appeals for one of the civil subdivisions of the State. His arguments lasted about a quarter of an hour. He told us his point and sat down. The audience in the rear of the court room might not applaud, but the audience in front did—at least in spirit—and since the latter audience has the votes, it is best to make your play for them. If you faithfully observe these cautions, let not your spirits droop too low when the decision is adverse, even though there be the added gall and wormwood of a failure of the court to crown your brilliant effort with the dignity of an opinion. Many a gallant argument has met the same unworthy fate.

Young men as they approach admission to the bar must sometimes say to themselves that the great problems have been solved, that the great battles of the forum have been fought, that the great opportunities are ended. There are moods in which for a moment I say the same thing to myself. If I do, the calendar of the following day is as likely as not to bring the exposure of the error. It is a false and cramping notion that cases are made great solely or chiefly by reason of something intrinsic in themselves. They are great by what we make of them. McCulloch *vs.* Maryland —to choose almost at random—is one of the famous cases of our history. I wonder, would it not be forgotten, and even perhaps its doctrine overruled, if Marshall had not put upon it the imprint of his genius. "Not one of his great opinions," says Professor Corwin, speaking of Marshall's work, "but might easily have been decided on comparatively narrow grounds in precisely the same way in which he decided it on broad, general principles, but with the probable result that it would never again have been heard of outside the law courts." So, too, the smaller issues await the transfiguring touch. "To a genuine accountant," says Charles Lamb, "the difference of proceeds is as nothing. The fractional farthing is as dear to his heart as the thousands which stand before it. He is the true actor, who, whether his part be a prince or a peasant, must act it with like authority." That is the spirit in which judge or advocate is to look upon his task. He is expounding a science, or a body of truth which he seeks to assimilate to a science, but in the process of exposition he is practicing an art. The Muses look at him a bit impatiently and wearily at times. He has done a good deal to alienate them, and sometimes they refuse to listen, and are seen to stop their ears. They have a strange capacity, however, for the discernment of strains of harmony and beauty, no matter how diffused and scattered through the ether. So at times when work is finely done, one sees their faces change, and they take the worker by the hand. They know that by the lever of art the subject the most lowly can be lifted to the heights. Small, indeed, is the company dwelling in those upper spaces, but the few are also the elect.

A MINISTRY OF JUSTICE[1]

THE courts are not helped as they could and ought to be in the adaptation of law to justice. The reason they are not helped is because there is no one whose business it is to give warning that help is needed. Time was when the remedial agencies, though inadequate, were at least in our own hands. Fiction and equity were tools which we could apply and fashion for ourselves. The artifice was clumsy, but the clumsiness was in some measure atoned for by the skill of the artificer. Legislation, supplanting fiction and equity, has multiplied a thousandfold the power and capacity of the tool, but has taken the use out of our own hands and put it in the hands of others. The means of rescue are near for the worker in

[1] Printed in the *Harvard Law Review*, Vol. XXXV, p. 113 ff., and in *Lectures on Legal Topics 1921–22*. By permission of the Harvard Law Review Association, publishers of the *Harvard Law Review*, and of the Macmillan Company, publishers of the *Lectures*, and also by permission of the Association of the Bar of the City of New York.

the mine. Little will the means avail unless lines of communication are established between the miner and his rescuer. We must have a courier who will carry the tidings of distress to those who are there to save when signals reach their ears. Today courts and legislature work in separation and aloofness. The penalty is paid both in the wasted effort of production and in the lowered quality of the product. On the one side, the judges, left to fight against anachronism and injustice by the methods of judge-made law, are distracted by the conflicting promptings of justice and logic, of consistency and mercy, and the output of their labors bears the tokens of the strain. On the other side, the legislature, informed only casually and intermittently of the needs and problems of the courts, without expert or responsible or disinterested or systematic advice as to the workings of one rule or another, patches the fabric here and there, and mars often when it would mend. Legislature and courts move on in proud and silent isolation. Some agency must be found to mediate between them.

This task of mediation is that of a ministry of justice. The duty must be cast on some man or group of men to watch the law in action, observe the manner of its functioning, and report the changes needed when function is deranged. The thought is not a new one. Among our own scholars, it has been developed by Dean Pound with fertility and power.[2] Others before him, as he reminds us, had seen the need, and urged it. Bentham made provision for such a ministry in his draft of a Constitutional Code.[3] Lord Westbury renewed the plea.[4] Only recently, Lord Haldane has brought it to the fore again.[5] "There is no functionary at present who can properly be called a minister responsible for the subject of Justice." [6] "We are impressed by the representations made by men of great experience, such as the President of the Incorporated Law Society,

[2] Pound, "Juristic Problems of National Progress," 22 *Am. J. of Sociology*, 721, 729, 731 (May, 1917); Pound, "Anachronisms in Law," 3 *J. Am. Judicature Soc.*, 142, 146 (February, 1920).

[3] *Works*, IX, 597–612.

[4] 1 *Nash, Life of Lord Westbury*, 191, quoted by Pound, *supra*.

[5] Report of Lord Haldane's Committee on the Machinery of Government (1918).

[6] *Ibid.*, p. 63.

as to the difficulty of getting the attention of the government to legal reform, and as to the want of contact between those who are responsible for the administration of the work of the Commercial Courts and the mercantile community, and by the evidence adduced that the latter are, in consequence and progressively, withdrawing their disputes from the jurisdiction of the Courts."[7] In countries of continental Europe, the project has passed into the realm of settled practice. Apart from these precedents and without thought of them, the need of such a ministry, of some one to observe and classify and criticize and report, has been driven home to me with steadily growing force through my own work in an appellate court. I have seen a body of judges applying a system of case law, with powers of innovation cabined and confined. The main lines are fixed by precedents. New lines may, indeed, be run, new courses followed, when precedents are lacking. Even then, distance and direction are guided by mingled considerations of logic and analogy and his-

[7] Report of Lord Haldane's Committee on the Machinery of Government (1918), p. 64.

tory and tradition which moderate and temper the promptings of policy and justice. I say this, not to criticize, but merely to describe. I have seen another body, a legislature, free from these restraints, its powers of innovation adequate to any need, preoccupied, however, with many issues more clamorous than those of courts, viewing with hasty and partial glimpses the things that should be viewed both steadily and whole. I have contrasted the quick response whenever the interest affected by a ruling untoward in results had some accredited representative, especially some public officer, through whom its needs were rendered vocal. A case involving, let us say, the construction of the Workmen's Compensation Law exhibits a defect in the statutory scheme. We find the Attorney General at once before the legislature with the request for an amendment. We cannot make a decision construing the tax law or otherwise affecting the finances of the state without inviting like results. That is because in these departments of the law there is a public officer whose duty prompts him to criticism and action.

Seeing these things, I have marveled and lamented that the great fields of private law, where justice is distributed between man and man, should be left without a caretaker. A word would bring relief. There is nobody to speak it.

For there are times when deliverance, if we are to have it—at least, if we are to have it with reasonable speed—must come to us, not from within, but from without. Those who know best the nature of the judicial process, know best how easy it is to arrive at an impasse. Some judge, a century or more ago, struck out upon a path. The course seemed to be directed by logic and analogy. No milestone of public policy or justice gave warning at the moment that the course was wrong, or that danger lay ahead. Logic and analogy beckoned another judge still farther. Even yet there was no hint of opposing or deflecting forces. Perhaps the forces were not in being. At all events, they were not felt. The path went deeper and deeper into the forest. Gradually there were rumblings and stirrings of hesitation and distrust, anxious glances were directed to the right and to the left, but the starting point was far behind, and there was no other path in sight.

Thus, again and again, the processes of judge-made law bring judges to a stand that they would be glad to abandon if an outlet could be gained. It is too late to retrace their steps. At all events, whether really too late or not, so many judges think it is that the result is the same as if it were. Distinctions may, indeed, supply for a brief distance an avenue of escape. The point is at length reached when their power is exhausted. All the usual devices of competitive analogies have finally been employed without avail. The ugly or antiquated or unjust rule is there. It will not budge unless uprooted. Execration is abundant, but execration, if followed by submission, is devoid of motive power. There is need of a fresh start; and nothing short of a statute, unless it be the erosive work of years, will supply the missing energy. But the evil of injustice and anachronism is not limited to cases where the judicial process, unaided, is incompetent to gain the mastery. Mastery, even when attained, is the outcome of a constant struggle in which logic and symmetry are sacrificed at times to equity and justice. The gain may justify the sacrifice; yet it is not gain without deduction. There is an attendant loss of that certainty which is itself a social asset. There is a loss too of simplicity and directness, an increasing aspect of unreality, of something artificial and fictitious, when judges mask a change of substance, or gloss over its importance, by the suggestion of a consistency that is merely verbal and scholastic. Even when these evils are surmounted, a struggle, of which the outcome is long doubtful, is still the price of triumph. The result is to subject the courts and the judicial process to a strain as needless as it is wearing. The machinery is driven to the breaking point; yet we permit ourselves to be surprised that at times there is a break. Is it not an extraordinary omission that no one is charged with the duty to watch machinery or output, and to notify the master of the works when there is need of replacement or repair?

In all this, I have no thought to paint the failings of our law in lurid colors of detraction. I have little doubt that its body is for the most part sound and pure. Not even its most zealous advocate, however, will assert that it is perfect. I do not seek to paralyze the inward forces, the "indwelling and creative" energies,[8] that make for its development and growth. My wish is rather to release them, to give them room and outlet for healthy and unhampered action. The statute that will do this, first in one field and then in others, is something different from a code, though, as statute follows statute, the material may be given from which in time a code will come. Codification is, in the main, restatement. What we need, when we have gone astray, is change. Codification is a slow and toilsome process, which, if hurried, is destructive. What we need is some relief that will not wait upon the lagging years. Indeed, a code, if completed, would not dispense with mediation between legislature and judges, for code is followed by commentary and commentary by revision, and thus the task is never done. "As in other sciences, so in politics, it is impossible

[8] 2 Bryce, *Studies in History and Jurisprudence*, 609.

that all things should be precisely set down in writing; for enactments must be universal, but actions are concerned with particulars." [9] Something less ambitious, in any event, is the requirement of the hour. Legislation is needed, not to repress the forces through which judge-made law develops, but to stimulate and free them. Often a dozen lines or less will be enough for our deliverance. The rule that is to emancipate is not to imprison in particulars. It is to speak the language of general principles, which, once declared, will be developed and expanded as analogy and custom and utility, and justice, when weighed by judges in the balance, may prescribe the mode of application and the limits of extension. The judicial process is to be set in motion again, but with a new point of departure, a new impetus and direction. In breaking one set of shackles, we are not to substitute another. We are to set the judges free.

I have spoken in generalities, but instances will leap to view. There are fields, known to us all,

[9] *Aristotle, Politics,* Bk. II (Jowett's translation).

where the workers in the law are hampered by rules that are outworn and unjust. How many judges, if they felt free to change the ancient rule, would be ready to hold today that a contract under seal may not be modified or discharged by another and later agreement resting in parol? [10] How many would hold that a deed, if it is to be the subject of escrow, must be delivered to a third person, and not to the grantee? [11] How many would hold that a surety is released, irrespective of resulting damage, if by agreement between principal and creditor the time of payment of the debt is extended for a single day? [12] How many would hold that a release of one joint tortfeasor is a release also of the others? How many would not prefer, instead of drawing some unreal distinction between releases under seal and covenants not to sue,[13] to extirpate, root and branch, a rule which is today an incumbrance and a

[10] 3 *Williston, Contracts*, §§ 1834–1837; Harris *vs.* Shorall, 230 N. Y. 343 (1921).

[11] Blewitt *vs.* Boorum, 142 N. Y. 357, 37 N. E. 119 (1894).

[12] N. Y. Life Ins. Co. *vs.* Casey, 178 N. Y. 381, 70 N. E. 916 (1904).

[13] Gilbert *vs.* Finch, 173 N. Y. 455, 66 N. E. 133 (1903); Walsh *vs.* N. Y. Central R. R. Co., 204 N. Y. 58, 97 N. E. 408 (1912); *cf.* 21 *Columbia L. Rev.* 491.

snare? How long would Pinnel's case[14] survive if its antiquity were not supposed to command the tribute of respect? How long would Dumpor's case[15] maintain a ghostly and disquieting existence in the ancient byways of the law?

I have chosen extreme illustrations as most likely to command assent. I do not say that judges are without competence to effect some changes of that kind themselves. The inquiry, if pursued, would bring us into a field of controversy which it is unnecessary to enter. Whatever the limit of power, the fact stares us in the face that changes are not made. But short of these extreme illustrations are others, less glaring and insistent, where speedy change is hopeless unless effected from without. Sometimes the inroads upon justice are subtle and insidious. A spirit or a tendency, revealing itself in a multitude of little things, is the evil to be remedied. No one of its manifestations is enough, when viewed alone, to spur the con-

[14] 5 Coke, 117; *cf.* Jaffray *vs.* Davis, 124 N. Y. 164, 167, 26 N. E. 351 (1891); Frye *vs.* Hubbell, 74 N. H. 358, 68 Atl. 325 (1907); 1 *Williston, Contracts*, § 121; *Anson, Contracts*, Corbin's ed., p. 137; Ferson, "The Rule in Foakes *vs.* Beer," 31 *Yale L. J.* 15.

[15] 2 Coke, 119.

science to revolt. The mischief is the work of a long series of encroachments. Examples are many in the law of practice and procedure.[16] At other times, the rule, though wrong, has become the cornerstone of past transactions. Men have accepted it as law, and have acted on the faith of it. At least, the possibility that some have done so, makes change unjust, if it were practicable, without saving vested rights. Illustrations again may be found in many fields. A rule for the construction of wills established a presumption that a gift to issue is to be divided, not *per stirpes*, but *per capita*.[17] The courts denounced and distinguished, but were unwilling to abandon.[18] In New York, a statute has at last released us from our bonds,[19] and we face the future unashamed. Still more common are the cases where the evil is less obvious, where there is room for difference of opinion,

[16] In jurisdictions where procedure is governed by rules of court, recommendations of the ministry affecting the subject-matter of the rules may be submitted to the judges.

[17] I state the law in New York and in many other jurisdictions. There are jurisdictions where the rule is different.

[18] Petry *vs.* Petry, 186 App. Div. 738, 175 N. Y. Supp. 30 (1919), 227 N. Y. 621, 125 N. E. 924 (1919); *Matter of Durant*, 231 N. Y. 41, 131 N. E. 562 (1921).

[19] Decedent's Estate Law, § 47a; L. 1921, c. 379.

where some of the judges believe that the existing rules are right, at all events where there is no such shock to conscience that precedents will be abandoned, and what was right declared as wrong. At such times there is need of the detached observer, the skillful and impartial critic, who will view the field in its entirety, and not, as judges view it, in isolated sections, who will watch the rule in its working, and not, as judges watch it, in its making, and who viewing and watching and classifying and comparing, will be ready, under the responsibility of office, with warning and suggestion.

I note at random, as they occur to me, some of the fields of law where the seeds of change, if sown, may be fruitful of results. Doubtless better instances can be chosen. My purpose is, not advocacy of one change or another, but the emphasis of illustration that is concrete and specific.

It is a rule in some jurisdictions that if A sends to B an order for goods, which C, as the successor to B's business, takes it on himself to fill, no action at the suit of C will lie either for the price or for the value, if A in accepting the goods and keeping them believed that they had been furnished to him by B, and this though C has acted without fraudulent intent.[20] I do not say that this is the rule everywhere. There are jurisdictions where the question is still an open one. Let me assume, however, a jurisdiction where the rule, as I have stated it, prevails, or even one where, because the question is unsettled, there is a chance that it may prevail. A field would seem to be open for the declaration by the lawmakers of a rule less in accord, perhaps, with the demands of a "jurisprudence of conceptions," [21] but more in accord with those of morality and justice. Many will prefer to turn to the principle laid down in the French Code Civil:

"L'erreur n'est une cause de nullité de la convention que lorsqu'elle tombe sur la substance même de la chose qui en est l'objet. Elle n'est point une cause de nullité, lorsqu'elle ne tombe

[20] Boulton *vs.* Jones, 2 H. & N. 564 (1857); 1 *Williston, Contracts*, § 80; *cf.* Boston Ice Co. *vs.* Potter, 123 Mass. 28 (1877); Kelly Asphalt Co. *vs.* Barber Asphalt Paving Co., 211 N. Y. 68, 71, 105 N. E. 88 (1914).

[21] Pound, "Mechanical Jurisprudence," 8 *Columbia L. Rev.* 605, 608, 610; Hynes *vs.* N. Y. Central R. R. Co., 231 N. Y. 229, 235, 131 N. E. 898 (1921).

que sur la personne avec laquelle on a intention de contracter, à moins que la considération de cette personne ne soit la cause principale de la convention."[22]

Much may be said for the view that in the absence of bad faith, there should be a remedy in quasi contract.[23]

It is a rule which has grown up in many jurisdictions and has become "a common ritual"[24] that municipal corporations are liable for the torts of employees if incidental to the performance or non-performance of corporate or proprietary duties, but not if incidental to the performance or non-performance of duties public or governmental. The dividing line is hard to draw.

"Building a drawbridge, maintaining a health department, or a charitable institution, confining and punishing criminals, assaults by policemen, operating an elevator in a city hall, driving an ambulance, sweeping and cleaning streets, have been held governmental acts. Sweeping and

[22] Code Civil, Art. 1110.

[23] *Anson Contracts* (Corbin's edition), 31; *Keener, Quasi Contracts,* 358–360.

[24] 34 *Harv. L. Rev.* 66.

cleaning streets, street lighting, operating electric light plants, or waterworks, maintaining prisons, have been held private functions."[25]

The line of demarcation, though it were plainer, has at best a dubious correspondence with any dividing line of justice. The distinction has been questioned by the Supreme Court of the United States.[26] It has been rejected recently in Ohio.[27] In many jurisdictions, however, as, for example in New York, it is supported by precedent so inveterate that the chance of abandonment is small. I do not know how it would fare at the hands of a ministry of justice. Perhaps such a ministry would go farther, and would wipe out, not merely the exemption of municipalities, but the broader exemption of the state.[28] At least there is a field for inquiry, if not for action.

It is a rule of law that the driver of an automobile or other vehicle who fails to look or listen for trains when about to cross a railroad, is guilty of

[25] 34 *Harv. L. Rev.* 67.
[26] Workmen *vs.* The Mayor, 179 U. S. 552, 574 (1900).
[27] Fowler *vs.* City of Cleveland, 100 Ohio St. 158, 126 N. E. 72 (1919).
[28] Smith *vs.* State, 227 N. Y. 405, 125 N. E. 841 (1920).

contributory negligence, in default, at least, of special circumstances excusing the omission. I find no fault with that rule. It is reasonable and just. But the courts in some jurisdictions have gone farther. They have held that the same duty that rests upon the driver rests also upon the passenger.[29] The friend whom I invite to ride with me in my car, and who occupies the rear seat beside me, while the car is in the care of my chauffeur, is charged with active vigilance to watch for tracks and trains, and is without a remedy if in the exuberance of jest or anecdote or reminiscence, he relies upon the vigilance of the driver to carry him in safety. I find it hard to imagine a rule more completely unrelated to the realities of life. Men situated as the guest in the case I have supposed do not act in the way that this rule expects and requires them to act. In the first place, they would in almost every case make the situa-

[29] Read *vs.* N. Y. C. & H. R. R. R. Co., 123 App. Div. 228, 107 N. Y. Supp. 1068 (1908); s. c., 165 App. Div. 910, 150 N. Y. Supp. 1108 (1914), aff'd., 219 N. Y. 660, 114 N. E. 1081 (1916); Noakes *vs.* N. Y. C. & H. R. R. R. Co., 121 App. Div. 716, 106 N. Y. Supp. 522 (1907), 195 N. Y. 543, 88 N. E. 1126 (1909). For the just rule see Weidlich *vs.* N. Y., N. H. & H. R. R., 93 Conn., 438, 106 Atl. 323 (1919); 31 *Yale L. J.* 101.

tion worse if they did; they would add bewilderment and confusion by contributing multitude of counsel. In the second place, they rightly feel that, except in rare emergencies of danger known to them, but unknown to the driver, it is not their business to do anything. The law in charging them with such a duty has shaped its rules in disregard of the common standards of conduct, the everyday beliefs and practices, of the average man and woman whose behavior it assumes to regulate. We must take a fresh start. We must erect a standard of conduct that realists can accept as just. Other fields of the law of negligence may be resurveyed with equal profit. The law that defines or seeks to define the distinction between general and special employers is beset with distinctions so delicate that chaos is the consequence. No lawyer can say with assurance in any given situation when one employment ends and the other begins. The wrong choice of defendants is often made, with instances, all too many, in which justice has miscarried.

Illustrations yet more obvious are at hand in

the law of evidence. Some of its rules are so unwieldy that many of the simplest things of life, transactions so common as the sale and delivery of merchandise, are often the most difficult to prove. Witnesses speaking of their own knowledge must follow the subject-matter of the sale from its dispatch to its arrival. I have been told by members of the bar that claims of undoubted validity are often abandoned, if contested, because the withdrawal of the necessary witnesses from the activities of business involves an expense and disarrangement out of proportion to the gain. The difficulty would be lessened if entries in books of account were admissible as *prima facie* evidence upon proof that they were made in the usual course of business. Such a presumption would harmonize in the main with the teachings of experience. Certainly it would in certain lines of business, as, *e.g.*, that of banking, where irregularity of accounts is unquestionably the rare exception. Even the books of a bank are not admissible at present without wearisome preliminaries.[30]

[30] Ocean Bank *vs.* Carll, 55 N. Y. 440 (1874); Bates *vs.* Preble, 151 U. S. 149 (1894).

In England, the subject has for many years been regulated by statute.[31] Something should be done in our own country to mitigate the hardship. "The dead hand of the common-law rule . . . should no longer be applied to such cases as we have here."[32]

We are sometimes slow, I fear, while absorbed in the practice of our profession, to find inequity and hardship in rules that laymen view with indignation and surprise. One can understand why this is so. We learned the rules in youth when we were students in the law schools. We have seen them reiterated and applied as truths that are fundamental and almost axiomatic. We have sometimes even won our cases by invoking them. We end by accepting them without question as part of the existing order. They no longer have the vividness and shock of revelation and discovery. There is need of conscious effort, of introspective moods and moments, before their moral quality

[31] 42 & 43 *Vict.*, c. 11; *Stephen, Digest of the Law of Evidence*, Art. 36.

[32] Rosen *vs.* United States, 245 U. S. 467 (1918). (The situation has been bettered in New York by a statute enacted since the writing of this paper. See Civil Practice Act, Sec. 374a, 1928.)

addresses itself to us with the same force as it does to others. This is at least one reason why the bar has at times been backward in the task of furthering reform. A recent study of the Carnegie Foundation for the Advancement of Teaching deals with the subject of training for the public profession of the law.[33] Dr. Pritchett says in his preface:[34]

"There is a widespread impression in the public mind that the members of the legal profession have not, through their organizations, contributed either to the betterment of legal education or to the improvement of justice to that extent which society has the right to expect."

The Centennial Memorial Volume of Indiana University contains a paper by the Dean of the Harvard Law School on the Future of Legal Education.[35]

"So long as the leaders of the bar," he says,[36] "do nothing to make the materials of our legal tradition available for the needs of the twentieth century, and our legislative lawmakers, more

[33] Bulletin No. 15, Carnegie Foundation.

[34] *Ibid.*, p. xvii.

[35] Pound, "The Future of Legal Education," 259.

[36] *Ibid.*, 268.

zealous than well instructed in the work they have to do, continue to justify the words of the chronicler—'the more they spake of law the more they did unlaw'—so long the public will seek refuge in specious projects of reforming the outward machinery of our legal order in the vain hope of curing its inward spirit."

Such reproaches are not uncommon. We do not need to consider either their justification or their causes. Enough for us that they exist. Our duty is to devise the agencies and stimulate the forces that will make them impossible hereafter.

What, then, is the remedy? Surely not to leave to fitful chance the things that method and system and science should order and adjust. Responsibility must be centered somewhere. The only doubt, it seems to me, is where. The attorneys-general, the law officers of the states, are overwhelmed with other duties. They hold their places by a tenure that has little continuity or permanence. Many are able lawyers, but a task so delicate exacts the scholar and philosopher, and scholarship and philosophy find precarious and doubtful nurture in the contentions of the bar. Even those qualities, however, are inadequate unless reënforced by others. There must go with them experience of life and knowledge of affairs. No one man is likely to combine in himself attainments so diverse. We shall reach the best results if we lodge power in a group, where there may be interchange of views, and where different types of thought and training will have a chance to have their say. I do not forget, of course, the work that is done by Bar Associations, state and national, as well as local, and by other voluntary bodies. The work has not risen to the needs of the occasion. Much of it has been critical rather than constructive. Even when constructive, it has been desultory and sporadic. No attempt has been made to cover with systematic and comprehensive vision the entire field of law. Discharge of such a task requires an expenditure of time and energy, a single-hearted consecration, not reasonably to be expected of men in active practice. It exacts, too, a scholarship and a habit of research not often to be found in those immersed in varied duties. Even if these objections were inadequate, the task ought not to be left to a number of voluntary committees, working at cross purposes. Recommendations would come with much greater authority, would command more general acquiescence on the part of legislative bodies, if those who made them were charged with the responsibilities of office. A single committee should be organized as a ministry of justice. Certain at least it is that we must come to some official agency unless the agencies that are voluntary give proof of their capacity and will to watch and warn and purge—unless the bar awakes to its opportunity and power.

How the committee should be constituted is, of course, not of the essence of the project. My own notion is that the ministers should be not less than five in number. There should be representatives, not less than two, perhaps even as many as three, of the faculties of law or political science in institutes of learning. Hardly elsewhere shall we find the scholarship on which the ministry must be able to draw if its work is to stand the test. There should be, if possible, a representative of the bench; and there should be a representative or representatives of the bar.

Such a board would not only observe for itself the workings of the law as administered day by day. It would enlighten itself constantly through all available sources of guidance and instruction; through consultation with scholars; through study of the law reviews, the journals of social science, the publications of the learned generally; and through investigation of remedies and methods in other jurisdictions, foreign and domestic. A project was sketched not long ago by John Bassett Moore, then Professor at Columbia University and later judge of the International Court, for an Institute of Jurisprudence.[37] It was to do for law what the Rockefeller Institute is doing for medicine. Such an institute, if founded, would be at the service of the ministers. The Commonwealth Fund has established a Committee for Legal Research which is initiating studies in branches of jurisprudence where reform may be

[37] Report of Dean of Columbia University Law School for 1916.

desirable. The results of its labors will be available for guidance. Professors in the universities are pointing the way daily to changes that will help. Professor Borchard of Yale by a series of articles on the Declaratory Judgment [38] gave the impetus to a movement which has brought us in many states a reform long waited for by the law.[39] Dean Stone of Columbia has disclosed inconsistencies and weaknesses in decisions that deal with the requirement of mutuality of remedy in cases of specific performance.[40] Professor Chafee in a recent article [41] has emphasized the need of reform in the remedy of interpleader. In the field of conflict of laws, Professor Lorenzen has shown disorder to the point of chaos in the rules that are supposed to regulate the validity and effect of contracts.[42] The archaic law of arbitration, amended not long ago in New York through the efforts of the Chamber of Commerce,[43] remains

[38] 28 *Yale L. J.* 1.
[39] 34 *Harv. L. Rev.* 697.
[40] The "Mutuality" Rule in New York, 16 *Columbia L. Rev.* 443.
[41] "Modernizing Interpleader," 30 *Yale L. J.* 814.
[42] 30 *Yale L. J.* 565, 655; 31 *id.*, 53.
[43] Matter of Berkovitz, 230 N. Y. 261, 130 N. E. 288 (1921).

in its archaic state in many other jurisdictions, despite requests for change. A ministry of justice will be in a position to gather these and like recommendations together, and report where change is needed. Reforms that now get themselves made by chance or after long and vexatious agitation, will have the assurance of considerate and speedy hearing. Scattered and uncoördinated forces will have a rallying point and focus. System and method will be substituted for favor and caprice. Doubtless, there will be need to guard against the twin dangers of overzeal on the one hand and of inertia on the other—of the attempt to do too much and of the willingness to do too little. In the end, of course, the recommendations of the ministry will be recommendations and nothing more. The public will be informed of them. The bar and others interested will debate them. The legislature may reject them. But at least the lines of communication will be open. The long silence will be broken. The spaces between the planets will at last be bridged.

The time is ripe for betterment. "Le droit a ses

époques," says Pascal in words which Professor Hazeltine has recently recalled to us. The law has "its epochs of ebb and flow." [44] One of the flood seasons is upon us. Men are insisting, as perhaps never before, that law shall be made true to its ideal of justice. Let us gather up the driftwood, and leave the waters pure.

[44] H. D. Hazeltine, 1 *Cambridge L. J.* 1.

WHAT MEDICINE CAN DO FOR LAW[1]

THERE are those who say that the earliest physician was the priest, just as the earliest judge was the ruler who uttered the divine command and was king and priest combined. Modern scholarship warns us to swallow with a grain of salt these sweeping generalities, yet they have at least a core of truth. Our professions—yours and mine—medicine and law—have divided with the years, yet they were not far apart at the beginning. There hovered over each the nimbus of a tutelage that was supernatural, if not divine. To this day each retains for the other a trace of the thaumaturgic quality distinctive of its origin. The physician is still the wonder-worker, the soothsayer, to whose reading of the entrails we resort when hard beset. We may scoff at him in health, but we send

[1] Address before The New York Academy of Medicine, November 1, 1928.

for him in pain. The judge, if you fall into his clutches, is still the Themis of the Greeks, announcing mystic dooms. You may not understand his words, but their effects you can be made to feel. Each of us is thus a man of mystery to the other, a power to be propitiated in proportion to the element within it that is mystic or unknown. "Speak not ill of a great enemy," says Selden in his *Table-Talk*—and Selden, you must know, was one of the ancient sages of our law—"speak not ill of a great enemy, but rather give him good words that he may use you the better if you chance to fall into his hands. The Spaniard did this when he was dying; his confessor told him, to work him to repentance, how the Devil tormented the wicked that went to hell; the Spaniard replying called the Devil my Lord; I hope my Lord the Devil is not so cruel. His confessor reproved him; excuse me for calling him so, says the Don, I know not into what hands I may fall, and if I happen into his, I hope he will use me the better for giving him good words." So with judges and doctors and devils it is all one, at least in hours of extremity.

One of these hours of extremity is at hand, the hour for the delivery of an anniversary address. The president of your Academy, moved I know not by what impulse—perhaps by some such faint foreboding as shaped the words of the Don in addressing his confessor—has turned with fair and soft speech to one without the mystic guild and has called upon a judge to preach the lesson of the hour. This is extraordinary enough, yet still more extraordinary is the fact that the judge has responded to the summons. In thus responding he has not been beguiled into the vain belief that any message he has to offer is worthy of your patience. He disclaims even a faint foreboding that there is need to propitiate your favor as against some future hour when he may be driven to seek your ministrations in default of other aid. Nothing is there on his side except a gesture of mere friendliness, the friendliness that is due between groups united in a common quest, the quest for the rule of order, the rule of health and of disease, to which for individuals as for society we give the name of law.

Indeed, the more I think it over, the more I feel the closeness of the tie that binds our guilds together. In all this there is nothing strange. I was reading the other day a very interesting document, a report to the overseers of Harvard University by the president of the university, Dr. A. Lawrence Lowell. He speaks of a new educational concept, the concept, as he calls it, of the continuity of knowledge. The idea is taking root that the subdivisions of science, like those of time itself, have been treated too often as absolute and genuine—that there is need to recognize them more fully as mere figments of the brain, mere labor-saving devices, helps to thinking, but like other helps to thinking, misleading if their origin is neglected or forgotten. Thus it is that the physicist is learning from the chemist, the zoölogist from the botanist, the economist from the statesman and the student of social science, the physician from the psychologist, and so on interchangeably and indefinitely. "The sharp severance," we are told, "is giving way, and we perceive that all subjects pass imperceptibly into others previously distinct." Something of this same concept of the continuity of knowledge is making its way into the law. In my own court at a recent session we had one case where a wise decision called for the wisdom of a chemist; another for that of one skilled in the science of mechanics; another for that of the student of biology and medicine; and so on through the list. I do not say we were able to supply this fund of wisdom out of the resources of our knowledge, yet in theory, at least, the litigants before us were entitled to expect it, and our efficiency as judges would be so much the greater, the quality of the output so much the sounder and richer, in proportion to our ability to make the theory one with fact. More and more we lawyers are awaking to a perception of the truth that what divides and distracts us in the solution of a legal problem is not so much uncertainty about the law as uncertainty about the facts—the facts which generate the law. Let the facts be known as they are, and the law will sprout from the seed and turn its branches toward the light. We make our blunders from time to time as rumor has it that you make your own. The worst of them would have been escaped if the facts had been disclosed to us before the ruling was declared. A statute of New York, forbidding night work for women, was declared arbitrary and void by a decision of the Court of Appeals announced in 1907.[2] In 1915, with fuller knowledge of the investigations of scientists and social workers, a like statute was held by the same court to be reasonable and valid.[2a] "Courts know today" (if I may borrow my own words) "that statutes are to be viewed, not in isolation or *in vacuo*, as pronouncements of abstract principles for the guidance of an ideal community, but in the setting and the framework of present-day conditions as revealed by the labors of economists and students of the social sciences in our own country and abroad."[3]

Examples to point the meaning come flocking at the call. Again and again we are asked to nullify legislation as an undue encroachment upon

[2] People *vs.* Williams, 189 N. Y. 131.

[2a] People *vs.* Schweinler Press, 214 N. Y. 395.

[3] Cardozo, *The Nature of the Judicial Process*, p. 81.

the sphere of individual liberty. Encroachment to some extent there is by every command or prohibition. Liberty in the literal sense is impossible for any one except the anarchist, and anarchy is not law, but its negation and destruction. What is undue in mandate or restraint cannot be known in advance of the event by a process of deduction from metaphysical principles of unvarying validity. It can be known only when there is knowledge of the mischief to be remedied, and knowledge of the mischief—to which, of course, must be added knowledge of the effectiveness of the remedy to counteract or cure the mischief—is knowledge of the facts. We do not turn to a body of esoteric legal doctrine, at least not invariably, to find the key to some novel problem of constitutional limitation, the bounds of permissible encroachment on liberty or property. We turn at times to physiology or embryology or chemistry or medicine—to a Jenner or a Pasteur or a Virchow or a Lister as freely and submissively as to a Blackstone or a Coke. Of course, even then we try to know our place and exhibit the humility that becomes the amateur. We do not assume to sit in judgment between conflicting schools of thought. Enough it is for us that the view embodied in a contested statute has at least respectable support —its sponsors, if perchance its critics—in the true abodes of science. Shall hours of labor be limited in one calling or another, for this group or for that? The physiologist as well as the sociologist must supply us with the body of knowledge appropriate to the problem to be solved. Such cases as People *vs.* The Schweinler Press [4] decided by the Court of Appeals of New York in 1915, and Muller *vs.* Oregon,[5] decided in 1908 by the Supreme Court of the United States, show the answer of the courts when the enlightening facts were put before them by workers in other fields. Shall compulsory vaccination be exacted of the children in the public schools? Read the answer of the courts in Matter of Viemeister,[6] decided in 1904, and Jacobson *vs.* Massachusetts,[7] decided a year later. Only the other day my court had to deal with the propriety of the tuberculin test as

[4] 214 N. Y. 395.
[5] 208 U. S. 412.
[6] 179 N. Y. 235.
[7] 197 U. S. 11.

applied to herds of cattle, the unfortunates who responded to the test being marked for quarantine or slaughter.[8] A question of scientific fact is at the core of other problems, juridical in form, and yet intense, or so I hear, in their emotional appeal. What is a beverage, and when is it intoxicating? Let me not open ancient wounds by a reminder of the answer.

We look then to you, to the students of mind and body, for the nutriment of fact, solid if not liquid, that in many a trying hour will give vitality and vigor to the tissues of our law. Conspicuously is this true today in the administration of the law of crime. The law of crime has dramatic features which make it bulk large in the public mind, though of all the cases in my court the criminal appeals make up a small proportion, say eight or ten per cent. None the less, from the viewpoint of its social consequences the criminal law has an importance that is imperfectly reflected in statistical averages or the tables of accountants. The field is one in which the physician is asserting

[8] People *vs.* Teuscher, July, 1928, 248 N. Y. 454.

himself year by year with steadily expanding power. Among students of criminology there are now many who maintain that the whole business of sentencing criminals should be taken away from the judges and given over to the doctors. Courts, with their judges and juries, are to find the fact of guilt or innocence. The fact being ascertained, the physician is to take the prisoner in hand and say what shall be done with him. Governor Smith in his message to the Legislature of 1928 recommended that this reform be studied by the Crime Commission. "Because," he said, "of my belief that justice sometimes miscarries because those charged with determining guilt are often affected by the thought of the sentence to be imposed for a given crime, I would suggest that the Crime Commission give careful study and consideration to a fundamental change in the method of sentencing criminals. After guilt has been determined by legal process, instead of sentence being fixed by judges according to statute, I should like to see offenders who have been adjudged guilty detained by the state. They should then be carefully studied by a board of expert mental and physical specialists, who after careful study of all the elements entering each case would decide and fix the penalty for the crime. I realize the complexity of such a fundamental change. It probably requires even constitutional amendment. Therefore I recommend that your honorable bodies request the Crime Commission to report to you, after due and careful study of the proposal, whether such a change is advisable and how it can be brought about. It appeals to me as a modern, humane, scientific way to deal with the criminal offender."

The reform thus proposed is no extemporized nostrum, no hasty innovation. It was recommended not many years ago by a committee of the Institute of Criminal Law and Criminology, of which the chairman was Victor P. Arnold, judge of the Juvenile Court of Chicago. This committee proposed *inter alia* "that in all cases of felony or misdemeanors punishable by a prison sentence the question of responsibility be not submitted to the jury, which will thus be called upon to determine only that the offense was committed by the defendant," and "that the disposition and treatment (including punishment) of all such misdemeanants and felons—*i.e.*, the sentence imposed, be based upon a study of the individual offender by properly qualified and impartial experts coöperating with the courts." [9] One of the most careful studies of the crime problem in recent years is that of Dr. S. Sheldon Glueck in his work on *Mental Disorder and the Criminal Law*. "If," he says,[10] "the socio-legal treatment of *all* criminals regardless of pathological condition were being considered, it would seem that the simplest device would be to permit the law to convict or acquit as is done today, but to provide for *an administrative* instrumentality (perhaps a commission composed of psychiatrists, psychologists, sociologists, and others) to begin to function in the case of convicted persons at the point where the law leaves off, to determine the appropriate socio-penal treatment adequate to the in-

[9] 10 *Journal Criminal Law and Criminology*, p. 186; Glueck, *Mental Disorder and the Criminal Law*, p. 455.

[10] Pp. 485, 486.

dividual delinquent, as well as its duration." Developing this thought in an interesting essay, "A Rational Penal Code," published in the *Harvard Law Review*,[11] he puts forward the view that the minimum sentence should be fixed by law, but that the maximum in every instance should be left indefinite, to be determined for the individual prisoner by psychiatrists and physicians after a study of the individual case (*cf.* Gillin, *Criminology and Penology*, p. 153). Even now in some of the countries of continental Europe—in Switzerland, for example—a criminal whose mentality is low, though insanity is not suspected, is turned over for examination to psychiatrists in the service of the government, who make their recommendations to the court before sentence is pronounced.[12]

Not a little impetus has been given to these and like reforms by researches of bio-chemists into the

[11] 41 *Harvard Law Review* 453.

[12] *Cf.* the recent statute of Massachusetts, 1. 1927, c. 59, which calls for an examination by psychiatrists of any person indicted for a capital offense or any person indicted for another offense after an earlier conviction for a felony. Such a statute will do much to remove the reproach that has attached so long and so persistently to the testimony of experts; see 13 *Mass. Law Quarterly*, p. 38, *et seq.*, No. 6, August, 1928.

operations of the ductless glands. If most of their conclusions are still in the stage of speculation or hypothesis, their writings have been useful, none the less, in awaking popular interest in the mentality of criminals, bringing home the need of study and the possibilities of a reformed penology to many who were blissfully unconscious of the existence of a problem. Our vices as well as our virtues have been imputed to bodily derangements till character has become identified with a chemical reaction. "The internal secretions," says an enthusiastic student of the endocrines,[13] "the internal secretions with their influence upon brain and nervous system, as well as every other part of the body-corporation, as essentially blood-circulating chemical substances, have been discovered the real governors and arbiters of instincts and dispositions, emotions and reactions, characters and temperaments, good and bad." A far cry is this from the voice of Socrates in the *Republic* of Plato: "My belief is, not that a good body will by its own excellence make the soul good; but, on

[13] Berman, *The Glands Regulating Personality*, p. 22.

the contrary, that a good soul will by *its* excellence render the body as perfect as it can be." The criminal of old was given copious draughts of exhortation and homily administered with solemn mien by reformers lay and cleric. The criminal of tomorrow will have fewer homilies and exhortations, but will have his doses of thyroxin or adrenalin till his being is transfigured. Good people sitting peacefully in their homes and reading fearsome tales of robbery and rapine, may take comfort in the thought that while the regeneration of character is in this process of "becoming," the body of the offender will be in the keeping of the law.

I have no thought in all this to express approval or disapproval of the project of withdrawing from the court the sentence-fixing power. One may see a wise reform there without acceptance of the creed that virtue and vice are not spiritual essences, but high-sounding synonyms for the hormones of the body. As to this last many of us, perhaps in our ignorance, will feel like echoing the words of Principal Jacks in his suggestive little book, *Constructive Citizenship*. "I think also," he says, "that while most of us are content to have our vices (but not our virtues) explained in this charitable manner by our neighbors, very few of us, and those the meanest, are in the habit of applying it to themselves. When we apply it to ourselves, a voice within seems to answer, 'It is false.'" He is speaking, as it happens, of another and earlier precept of criminology, the precept that virtue and vice are the products solely of environment; but his words are as apposite to the notion that they are the products chiefly of the glands, though in each case it is true that repugnance must not be taken as amounting to disproof. All this, however, is beside the mark, at least for present purposes. Like the neophytes of other faiths, the discoverers of the new theory that virtue and vice are synonyms for spontaneous secretions may have overshot the mark, may have loaded a useful notion with more than it can bear. To prove that genius is accompanied by certain bodily changes or reactions is not to prove that the bodily changes or reactions are identical with genius.* This does not detract from the fullness of my belief that at a day not far remote the teachings of bio-chemists and behaviorists, of psychiatrists and penologists, will transform our whole system of punishment for crime. Vain is the attempt to forecast here and now the lines of the transfigured structure. We must keep a sharp lookout, or you will supplant us altogether. Do they not tell the fable of Hippocrates that he burned the library of the Temple of Health at Cnidus in order to enjoy a monopoly of knowledge? How it will work out, whether we shall sit beside you or above you, or even perhaps below you, I am not wise enough to say. The physician may be merely the ally of the judge in the business of admeasuring the sentence, or, as to that branch of the work, may even drive the judge away. Detention of the offender may retain in respect of certain crimes the qualities, or some of them, belonging to our present system of imprisonment, and for other crimes may acquire a quality less punitive and rigorous. But transformation there will be.

* *Cf.* Bertrand Russell, *Philosophy*, p. 218.

For the present system is stern often when it should be mild, and mild often when it should be stern, or so, at least, its critics urge. It is a survival of the time when punishment for crime was thought of as a substitute for private vengeance, with its sequel private war. The familiar phrase, the King's Peace, means this and nothing more, that for the peace separately maintained by duke or count or bishop, each in his own domain, there was to be substituted one general or uniform peace, the king's, establishing a single rule throughout the kingdom far and wide. You will find it all set forth by Sir Frederick Pollock in one of his fascinating essays with the fullness of example that is dear to antiquarians.[14] We have put away the blood feud, the vendetta, the other forms of private war, but in the framing of our penal codes we have not forgotten the passions that had their outlet and release in pursuit and retribution. I do not say that it is wise to forget them altogether. The thirst for vengeance is a very real, even if it be a hideous, thing; and states

[14] Pollock, Oxford Lectures, *The King's Peace*, p. 64.

may not ignore it till humanity has been raised to greater heights than any that have yet been scaled in all the long ages of struggle and ascent. Disregard such passions altogether, and the alternative may be the recrudescence of the duel or the feud. The vigilance committee and Judge Lynch may shove aside police and courts. Even if vengeance be forgotten and the social consequences alone considered, there are inhibitions in the threat of punishment that society cannot afford to withdraw from any capable of feeling them. "The presence of mechanism," says Dr. Glueck,[15] "does not mean that human beings have not some spark of capacity for consciously and creatively guiding their conduct in conformity with legal sanctions." Punishment is necessary, indeed, not only to deter the man who is a criminal at heart, who has felt the criminal impulse, who is on the brink of indecision, but also to deter others who in our existing social organization have never felt the criminal impulse and shrink from crime in horror. Most of us have such a scorn and loathing

[15] *Op. cit.*, p. 444.

of robbery or forgery that the temptation to rob or forge is never within the range of choice; it is never a real alternative. There can be little doubt, however, that some of this repugnance is due to the ignominy that has been attached to these and like offenses through the sanctions of the criminal law. If the ignominy were withdrawn, the horror might be dimmed.

All this I have in mind, yet even so, the present system, in the view of many, is as irrational in its mercies as in its rigors, and in its rigors as in its mercies. The casual offender expiates his offense in the company of defectives and recidivists, and after devastating years is given back an outcast to the society that made him. The defective or recidivist, whose redemption is hopeless, goes back after a like term, or one not greatly different, to renew his life of crime, unable to escape it without escaping from himself. Students of the mind and body are insisting, as never before, that in much of our criminology there is futility and waste. "It is foolish," says one of them, "to build institutions for detaining defectives for long periods as a punishment for a condition for which they are not responsible, and then discharge them without doing anything to remove the cause of their trouble." "For a large proportion of criminals," says another author, "—the percentage has yet to be determined—punishment for a period of time and then letting him go free is like imprisoning a diphtheria-carrier for a while and then permitting him to commingle with his fellows and spread the germ of diphtheria." [16] A beginning of a change has been made in this state by recent legislation, but with tests, in the thought of many, too mechanical and absolute. Not improbably the path of progress has been marked in an English statute which supplements the term of punishment in prison with another and elastic term of what is known as preventive detention in less rigorous surroundings, a camp in the Isle of Wight being set aside for that use.[17]

[16] S. W. Bandler, *The Endocrines*, p. 266; Berman, *The Glands Regulating Personality*, p. 310; Schlapp and Smith, *The New Criminology*, p. 270.

[17] Gillin, *Criminology and Penology*, p. 412; Preventive of Crime Act, 8 Edw. 7 c. 59; Halsbury Laws of England, Title Crim. L., § 796.

On the same lines a recent amendment of the Prison Law of New York permits the detention of mental defectives at the State Institution at Napanoch after sentence has expired (Prison Law, §§ 467, 470; Laws of

Here or in some system not dissimilar may be found the needed adjustment between the penal and the remedial elements in our scheme of criminology.

Adjustment of some sort there must be if we are to fill the measure of our duty to our defective fellow beings. Run your eyes over the life history of a man sentenced to the chair. There, spread before you in all its inevitable sequence, is a story of the Rake's Progress more implacable than any that was ever painted by a Hogarth. The Correctional School, the Reformatory, Sing Sing or Dannemora, and then at last the chair. The heavy hand of doom was on his head from the beginning. The sin, in truth, is ours—the sin of a penal system that leaves the victim to his fate when the course that he is going is written down so plainly in the files of the courts and the stigmata of mind and body. I do not mean to say that any rule of thumb is to be adopted in dealing with these problems.

1927, chap. 426), but the term mental defectives as used in the statute (Mental Hygiene Law, § 136) embraces a narrower class than the same term is meant to embrace as it is used in this address. Very likely an extension of these provisions to prisoners of other types may be expected in the future.

My experience as a judge in other fields of law has made me distrustful of rules of thumb generally. They are a lazy man's expedient for ridding himself of the trouble of thinking and deciding. Try hard as we will, the problems of punishment, like the problems of law generally, are in their essence unique. "We must spread the gospel," writes Professor Powell, "we must spread the gospel that there is no gospel that will save us from the pain of choosing at every step." Human nature, like human life, has complexities and diversities too many and too intricate to be compressed within a formula. I would not shut the door of hope on any one, though classified in some statistical table as defective or recidivist, so long as scientific analysis and study of his mental and physical reactions after the state had taken him in hand held out the promise of redemption. Neither in punishment nor in any other form of judging shall we ever rid ourselves altogether of the heartbreaking burden of individual adjustment.

I do not say that either psychology or medicine or penology has yet arrived at such a stage as to make a revolution in our system of punishment advisable or possible. Here as in so many fields we shall have to feel our way, it may be, by slow advances, by almost insensible approaches. I have faith, none the less, that a century or less from now, our descendants will look back upon the penal system of today with the same surprise and horror that fill our own minds when we are told that only about a century ago one hundred and sixty crimes were visited under English law with the punishment of death, and that in 1801 a child of thirteen was hanged at Tyburn for the larceny of a spoon.[18] Dark chapters are these in the history of law. We think of them with a shudder, and say to ourselves that we have risen to heights of mercy and of reason far removed from such enormities. The future may judge us less leniently than we choose to judge ourselves.[19] Perhaps the whole business of the retention of the death penalty will seem to the next generation, as it seems to many even now, an anachronism too

[18] 4 Blackstone, Comm. 18; *cf.* however, 1 Stephen, *History of the Criminal Law of England* 470.

[19] *Cf.* Jung, *Das Problem des Natürlichen Rechts*, p. 74.

discordant to be suffered, mocking with grim reproach all our clamorous professions of the sanctity of life. Perhaps some new Howard will make us see in our whole prison system a reproach as great, a blot as dark, as the Howard of English history made visible to the eyes of all in the prisons and pest houses of a century and a half ago. I am not sure how this will be. Sure, however, I am that whatever enlightenment shall come will make its way, not through the unaided labors of the men of my profession, the judges and the advocates, but through the combined labors of men of many callings, and most of all your own. How quickly a great change can come about will be seen if we contrast the penal justice applied to children a quarter-century ago with the treatment in these days of the juvenile delinquent by the judges of the Children's Courts. You will find it all set forth in a recent study of Juvenile Courts in the United States by Dr. Herbert H. Lou in the Social Study Series of the University of North Carolina. The methods, the humane and scientific methods, that have thus prevailed will spread to other fields. This is your work, I am persuaded, as much as it is ours. Your hands must hold the torch that will explore the dark mystery of crime —the mystery, even darker, of the criminal himself, in all the deep recesses of thought and will and body. Here is a common ground, a borderland between your labors and our own, where hope and faith and love can do their deathless work.

One takes a large order when one offers to reshape from its foundations a scheme of penal justice. Those of us whose course has even now been largely run, may wish to have before us a prospect less Utopian. Let me call attention, therefore, to two features of the law of crimes where the coöperation of your profession will be helpful even now without wreaking our energies upon reforms that will flower at some distant day. I think the men of your Academy might well emphasize the need for a restatement of our law of homicide, and in particular of the distinction between murder in its two degrees. I think they might well emphasize another subject—one that has grown a trifle stale, but never to be abandoned till it has been settled right—the definition of insanity when viewed as an excuse for crime.

The law of homicide, and in particular the distinction between murder in the first and second degrees, may seem at first blush to be something that involves the mere technique of criminal law, and so a matter not for you, but one to be dealt with by the lawyers. The reason why I mention it to you is because the anomalies of the present distinction can be developed with special clearness and authority by the psychiatrist or the alienist or the student of psychology.

Homicide under our statute is classified as murder and as manslaughter, and murder itself has two degrees, a first and a second. "The killing of a human being, unless it is excusable or justifiable, is murder in the first degree when committed from a deliberate and premeditated design to effect the death of the person killed, or of another," as well as in certain other situations which, for the purpose of my present inquiry, it is not important to consider.[20] "Such killing of a

[20] Penal Law, § 1044.

human being is murder in the second degree, when committed with a design to effect the death of the person killed or of another, but without deliberation and premeditation."[21] There, you see, is the distinction, and it is at least verbally clear. Both first and second degree murder (laying aside the exceptions which I thought it unnecessary to state) require an intent to kill, but in the one instance it is deliberate and premeditated intent, and in the other it is not. If there is no intent to kill whatever, the grade (subject to exceptions) is reduced to manslaughter. I have said that on the face of the statute the distinction is clear enough. The difficulty arises when we try to discover what is meant by the words deliberate and premeditated. A long series of decisions, beginning may years ago, has given to these words a meaning that differs to some extent from the one revealed upon the surface. To deliberate and premeditate within the meaning of the statute, one does not have to plan the murder days or hours or even minutes in advance, as

[21] Penal Law, § 1046.

where one lies in wait for one's enemy or places poison in his food and drink. The law does not say that any particular length of time must intervene between the volition and the act. The human brain, we are reminded,[22] acts at times with extraordinary celerity. All that the statute requires is that the act must not be the result of immediate or spontaneous impulse. "If there is hesitation or doubt to be overcome, a choice made as the result of thought, however short the struggle between the intention and the act," there is such deliberation and premeditation as will expose the offender to the punishment of death.[23] Thus in a case decided in 1886,[24] the defendant ejected a trespasser; a fight ensued; the defendant stabbed the trespasser and flung him to the ground; having done this, he seized an ax and clove the victim's head. The interval between the knife blow and the falling ax was long enough to sustain the verdict that sent the murderer to his death. One may say indeed in a rough way that an intent to

[22] People *vs.* Majone, 91 N. Y. 211.
[23] People *vs.* Leighton, 88 N. Y. 117.
[24] People *vs.* Beckwith, 103 N. Y. 360.

kill is always deliberate and premeditated within the meaning of the law unless the mind is so blinded by pain or rage as to make the act little more than an automatic or spontaneous reaction to the environment—not strictly automatic or spontaneous, for there could then be no intent, and yet a near approach thereto. The behaviorists would say, I suppose, that what had happened was a conditioned reflex, a learned, as opposed to an unlearned, response.[25] Courts in other states (*e.g.*, Massachusetts) lay down the same rules or rules not greatly different.

I think the distinction is much too vague to be continued in our law. There can be no intent unless there is a choice, yet by the hypothesis, the choice without more is enough to justify the inference that the intent was deliberate and premeditated. The presence of a sudden impulse is said to mark the dividing line, but how can an impulse be anything but sudden when the time for its formation is measured by the lapse of seconds? Yet the decisions are to the effect that seconds

[25] Watson, *Behaviorism*, p. 103, and *cf.* B. Russell, *Philosophy*, p. 21.

may be enough. What is meant, as I understand it, is that the impulse must be the product of an emotion or passion so swift and overmastering as to sweep the mind from its moorings. A metaphor, however, is, to say the least, a shifting test whereby to measure degrees of guilt that mean the difference between life and death. I think the students of the mind should make it clear to the lawmakers that the statute is framed along the lines of a defective and unreal psychology. If intent is deliberate and premeditated whenever there is choice, then in truth it is always deliberate and premeditated, since choice is involved in the hypothesis of the intent. What we have is merely a privilege offered to the jury to find the lesser degree when the suddenness of the intent, the vehemence of the passion, seems to call irresistibly for the exercise of mercy. I have no objection to giving them this dispensing power, but it should be given to them directly and not in a mystifying cloud of words. The present distinction is so obscure that no jury hearing it for the first time can fairly be expected to assimilate and understand it. I am not at all sure that I understand it myself after trying to apply it for many years and after diligent study of what has been written in the books. Upon the basis of this fine distinction with its obscure and mystifying psychology, scores of men have gone to their death. I think it is time for you who speak with authority as to the life of the mind to say whether the distinction has such substance and soundness that it should be permitted to survive. Some appropriate committee there should be in the bar associations, on the one hand, and this Academy, on the other (if none exists already), whereby the resources of the two professions can be pooled in matters such as these where society has so much to gain from coöperative endeavor.

I have spoken of another branch of the law of homicide, the law defining and governing mental irresponsibility. In strictness, this is not a branch of the law of homicide alone, since the same definition applies to other crimes as well, yet it is in connection with homicide that the question commonly arises. In the early stages of our law, way back in medieval times, insanity was never a defense for crime. The insane killer, like the man who killed in self-defense, might seek a pardon from the king, and would often get one. He had no defense at law. Gradually there came in the law itself a mitigation of this rigor. A defense of insanity was allowed, but only within the narrowest limits. This was what has become known as the wild-beast stage of the defense. The killer was not excused unless he had so lost his mind as to be no more capable of understanding than if he were merely a wild beast. Then the limits of the defense were expanded, but still slowly and narrowly. The killer was excused if the disease of the mind was such that he was incapable of appreciating the difference between right and wrong. At first this meant, not the right and wrong of the particular case, but right and wrong generally or in the abstract, the difference, as it was sometimes said, between good and evil. Later the rule was modified in favor of the prisoner so that capacity to distinguish between right and wrong generally would not charge with responsibility if there was not capacity to understand the difference in relation to the particular act, the subject of the crime. The rule governing the subject was crystallized in England in 1843 by the answer made by the House of Lords to questions submitted by the judges in the famous case of McNaghten, who was tried for the murder of one Drummond, the secretary of Sir Robert Peel. The answer was in effect that "the jurors ought to be told in all cases that every man is to be presumed to be sane, and to possess a sufficient degree of reason to be responsible for his crimes, until the contrary be proved to their satisfaction; and that to establish a defense on the ground of insanity it must be clearly proved that, at the time of committing the act, the accused was laboring under such a defect of reason from disease of the mind, as not to know the nature and quality of the act he was doing, or, if he did know it, that he did not know he was doing what was wrong." [26]

The test established by McNaghten's Case has been incorporated into the law of New York by

[26] McNaghten's Case, 10 Cl. & F. 200.

the mandate of the statute. Penal Law, § 34, provides: "A person is not excused from criminal liability as an idiot, imbecile, lunatic or insane person, except upon proof that at the time of the commission of the alleged criminal act he was laboring under such a defect of reason as either (1) not to know the nature and quality of the act he was doing; (2) not to know the act was wrong." It matters not that some uncontrollable impulse, the product of mental disease, may have driven the defendant to the commission of the murderous act. The law knows nothing of such excuses.[27] Again the statute is explicit: "A morbid propensity to commit prohibited acts, existing in the mind of a person who is not shown to have been incapable of knowing the wrongfulness of such acts, forms no defense to a prosecution therefor." [28] If the offender knew the nature and quality of the act and knew it to be wrong, he must answer for it with his life, if death is the penalty that would be paid by the sane. Of course, there is an am-

[27] Flanagan *vs.* People, 52 N. Y. 467; People *vs.* Carpenter, 102 N. Y. 238; People *vs.* Taylor, 138 N. Y. 398.

[28] Penal Law, § 34.

biguity in all this which will not have escaped your quick discernment. What is meant by knowledge that the act is wrong? Is it enough that there was knowledge that the act was wrong in the sense that it was prohibited by law, or must there be knowledge also that it was morally wrong? Curiously enough, this question did not arise in New York till 1915. One Schmidt, a priest, was charged with the murder of a woman with whom he had been intimate. Upon the trial his defense was insanity. He said he had heard the voice of God calling upon him by day and night to sacrifice and slay. He yielded to the call in the belief that slaughter was a moral duty. The trial judge held that this belief was no defense if he knew the nature of the act and knew it to be wrong in the sense of being prohibited by law. On appeal this ruling was reversed.[29] We held that the word "wrong" in the statutory definition had reference in such circumstances to the moral quality of the act, and not merely to the legal prohibition. Any other reading would charge a mother with the

[29] People *vs.* Schmidt, 216 N. Y. 324.

crime of murder if she were to slay a dearly loved child in the belief that a divine command had summoned to the gruesome act. Let me say by way of parenthesis that Schmidt did not profit by the error in the charge, since he admitted under oath that the whole defense of insanity was an imposture and a sham.

Physicians time and again rail at the courts for applying a test of mental responsibility so narrow and inadequate. There is no good in railing at us. You should rail at the legislature. The judges have no option in the matter. They are bound, hand and foot, by the shackles of a statute. Every one concedes that the present definition of insanity has little relation to the truths of mental life. There are times, of course, when a killing has occurred without knowledge by the killer of the nature of the act. A classic instance is the case of Mary Lamb, the sister of Charles Lamb, who killed her mother in delirium. There are times when there is no knowledge that the act is wrong, as when a mother offers up her child as a sacrifice to God. But after all, these are rare instances of the workings of a mind deranged. They exclude many instances of the commission of an act under the compulsion of disease, the countless instances, for example, of crimes by paranoiacs under the impulse of a fixed idea. I am not unmindful of the difficulty of framing a definition of insanity that will not be so broad as to open wide the door to evasion and imposture. Conceivably the law will have to say that the risk is too great, that the insane must answer with their lives, lest under cover of their privilege the impostor shall escape. Conceivably the twilight zone between sanity and insanity is so broad and so vague as to bid defiance to exact description. I do not know, though I am reluctant to concede that science is so impotent. Attempts at formulation of a governing principle or standard have been none too encouraging,[30] but betterment is attainable, though it be something less than perfection. Many states—Massachusetts, for example, and Alabama and Pennsylvania and Virginia and Vermont—recognize the fact that insanity may find expression in an

[30] Glueck, *op. cit.*, pp. 452, 459.

irresistible impulse, yet I am not aware that the administration of their criminal law has suffered as a consequence.[31] Much of the danger might be obviated if the issue of insanity were triable by a specially constituted tribunal rather than the usual jury. Of this at least I am persuaded: the medical profession of the state, the students of the life of the mind in health and in disease, should combine with students of the law in a scientific and deliberate effort to frame a definition, and a system of administration, that will combine efficiency with truth. If insanity is not to be a defense, let us say so frankly and even brutally, but let us not mock ourselves with a definition that palters with reality. Such a method is neither good morals nor good science nor good law. I know it is often said, and very likely with technical correctness,[32] that the statute ought not to be viewed as defining insanity. What it does, and all that it does is to state the forms or phases of in-

[31] See, *e.g.*, Commonwealth *vs.* Cooper, 219 Mass. 1; Parsons *vs.* State, 81 Ala. 577; Commonwealth *vs.* DeMarzo, 223 Pa. St. 573; State *vs.* Dejarnette, 75 Va. 867; Doherty *vs.* State, 73 Vt. 380.

[32] See *e.g.*, Oppenheimer, *Criminal Responsibility of Lunatics*, p. 247; Stephen, *Digest of Criminal Law*, Art. 29; Glueck, *op. cit.*, p. 43.

sanity that will bring immunity from punishment. All this may be true, yet it is hard to read the statute without feeling that by implication and suggestion it offers something more. It keeps the word of promise to the ear and breaks it to the hope. Let us try to improve its science and at the very least its candor. Here is another field for the coöperative endeavor of medicine and law.

Every now and then there crops up in popular journals a discussion of the problem of euthanasia. The query is propounded whether the privilege should be accorded to a physician of putting a patient painlessly out of the world when there is incurable disease, agonizing suffering, and a request by the sufferer for merciful release. No such privilege is known to our law, which shrinks from any abbreviation of the span of life, shaping its policy in that regard partly under the dominance of the precepts of religion and partly in the fear of error or abuse. Just as a life may not be shortened, so its value must be held as equal to that of any other, the mightiest or the lowliest. The mother will have the preference over an infant yet unborn, but from the moment of birth onward, humankind, as the law views it, is a society of equals. I am sure that thoughts of this order must rise sometimes to your minds when you move along the wards of hospitals and see the forms of men and women—the ugly and the beautiful, the wise and the foolish, the young and the old, the gay and the wretched—outstretched before you in the great democracy of suffering. You may find it of some interest to be told that the law has had to struggle with these problems and to know how it has resolved them. There are two classic cases—the case of the U. S. *vs.* Holmes, reported in 1 Wallace, Jr., 1; Federal cases No. 15,383, a trial in the United States Circuit Court for the Eastern District of Pennsylvania, and the case of the Queen *vs.* Dudley, reported in L. R. 14 Q. B. D. 273, a trial in the Court of Queen's Bench of England. The Holmes case has recently been revived with a full statement of the testimony, the arguments of counsel, and the charge of the court in a book by Frederick C. Hicks, to which he has given the title *Human Jettison.* Any of you who care to read it will find a human document of absorbing interest. Holmes was a seaman on a ship, the *William Brown*, which set sail from Liverpool for Philadelphia in 1841 with eighty-two souls aboard, seventeen officers and crew, and sixty-five passengers. Thirty-seven days out the ship struck an iceberg and sank. Two boats were lowered. One, the jolly, as it was called, bore the captain, two officers, six members of the crew, and one passenger. Six days later, just as the rations had given out, she was picked up and those aboard her saved. The other boat, styled the long one, in the charge of the first mate, had forty-two aboard, of whom thirty-three were passengers, the others crew. The long boat was long only by comparison with the other. She was overweighted with her human burden—men, women and children packed so close together in a boat already leaking that they could hardly move a limb. A squall came up the next day, and imminent was the danger that the boat would founder. The mate gave the order to jettison a portion of the human freight. Holmes and another carried out the mandate. Fourteen men were seized and, amid their protests and entreaties, were thrown over the side. Two women also were lost, but there is reason to believe that they jumped overboard of their own will, made desperate at the sight of the sacrifice of a brother. For the most part, however, the victims were the men. The boat, relieved of this burden, rode the waves in safety. The following morning a sail was sighted. Quilts and blankets were waved and hoisted. There was an answer to the signal. The ship came up and the remnant on the boat were saved.

When the story of the sacrifice of sixteen souls became known to the world, there were many who drew back revolted and said that it was murder. The mate and most of the seamen disappeared when there was talk of an arrest. Holmes came to Philadelphia and was charged with homicide on the high seas, a crime under the federal law. The grand jury refused to indict for murder, but did indict for manslaughter. For this he was tried and convicted. He was sentenced to imprisonment for six months, having already served nine months before his conviction, and also to a fine, which, however, was afterward remitted. I think there is little, if any, doubt that he had acted in good faith, believing that all would be lost unless there was a sacrifice of some. His good faith did not purge him of the guilt of crime, though it called for mercy in the sentence. Where two or more are overtaken by a common disaster, there is no right on the part of one to save the lives of some by the killing of another. There is no rule of human jettison. Men there will often be who, when told that their going will be the salvation of the remnant, will choose the nobler part and make the plunge into the waters. In that supreme moment the darkness for them will be illumined by the thought that those behind will ride to safety. If none of such mold are found aboard the boat, or too few to save the others, the human freight must be left to meet the chances of the waters. Who shall choose in such an hour between the victims and the saved? Who shall know when masts and sails of rescue may emerge out of the fog?

A score of years later a case not dissimilar was

brought before an English court. Three men and a boy were adrift in a small boat. Two of the men, Dudley and Stephens, made desperate by hunger, killed the boy and ate his flesh. Four days later they were picked up by a passing vessel, and, reaching England, were tried for murder. They were tried before an accomplished judge, Lord Coleridge, Chief Justice of the Queen's Bench. The jury returned a verdict of guilty, but the sentence of death was commuted to one of imprisonment for a term of months. The law falters and averts her face and sheathes her own sword when pronouncing judgment upon creatures of flesh and blood thus goaded by the Furies.

One thing medicine has already done for jurisprudence, and that a thing so important as to exact a word of mention in even the briefest statement of the relations between the two. For many years medicine has been laying stress upon the value of institutes of mere research. You will find a sketch of their history in Dr. Abraham Flexner's *Study of Medical Education*. The law has been a little slower in the acceptance of such methods and ideals, yet at last it has seen the light. I cannot doubt that your example has done much to open our eyes and sharpen our perceptions. Research is now the cry in the schools of law at Harvard, Yale, Columbia, Michigan, and elsewhere. They are seeking to train the practitioner who some day may develop, or shall I say descend, into a judge, but they are seeking to do more. They are seeking to train the scholars—the jurists in the true sense of that much-abused term—who will lead the vanguard of the march. Only the other day, Johns Hopkins University, which has done so much already to stimulate the growth of medicine, announced the formation of an Institute of Jurisprudence, devoted to research and nothing else. A group of scholars has been brought together, who at the beginning will have no pupils other than themselves. They have come together to meditate, to confer, to collate, to explore. They will study the law functionally, asking themselves not merely whether this or that rule has come down to us from medieval days, but whether this rule or that one is adapted to the present needs of life. So the spirit of disinterested inquiry, which has long inspired the students of the physical sciences, is spreading, we may justly believe, to the social sciences as well. I do not mean to convey the thought that the law which is mere innovation, a forced plant, so to speak, without roots in habit or custom or popular conviction, is to be looked to with great hopefulness as a curative or helpful force. What I fear and would avoid is the law that maintains a noxious life when the soil of habit and custom and conviction and utility has been washed away beneath it. I have no delusions as to the futility of mere extempore decretals. Even when changes are made, it is best at the beginning to mark out the general lines of tendency and direction, leaving details to be developed by the system of trial and error which is of the essence of the judicial process. "It is a peculiar virtue of our system of law"—the words are those of one of the great judges of our day—"that the process of inclusion and exclusion, so often employed in developing a rule, is not allowed to end with its enunciation, and that an expression in an opinion yields later to the impact of facts unforeseen."[33] We must not sacrifice this quality of resilient adaptability which persists while there is softness and suppleness in the bones of legal doctrine. I do not say that it is an easy matter to find a just mean between timidity and boldness, or, to put it from another aspect, between literature and dogma. In case of doubt I have a leaning, which is not always shared by others, toward the impressionism that suggests and illumines without defining and imprisoning. The prevailing tendency is perhaps the other way, and the majority may be right. They hold the mysticism of the impressionist to be incompatible with the dignity of science. I am satisfied that this is so when science has so experimented as to have the right to be certain of its ground. What I fear is a pseudo-science which has assurance without conviction. Very likely in this mental attitude I am exemplifying what has been described by a learned author as "the invertebrate habit of mind which thinks it

[33] Brandeis, J., dissenting, in Jaybird Mining Co. *vs.* Weir, 271 U.S. 609.

is impartial merely because it is undecided, and regards the judicial attitude as that which refrains from judging."[34] When the seas are so boisterous and their perils so insidious, one creeps from cape to cape.

The law, like medicine, has its record of blunders and blindness and superstitions and even cruelties. Like medicine, however, it has never lacked the impulse of a great hope, the vision of a great ideal. Sometimes secreted in ancient forms and ceremonies one finds the inner life and meaning of an institution revealed in all its essence. I felt this not long ago while reading the form of oath administered even now in all its ancient beauty to the grand jurors of the county. You will find it in the Code of Criminal Procedure, but one not greatly different is in use by our English brethren in their home across the seas, and Sir Frederick Pollock has traced it back, in germ at least, to the days of the Saxon kings. In fitness and beauty and impressiveness it rivals the great oath

[34] Dr. Figgis, Introduction to Lord Acton's *The History of Freedom and Other Essays*.

that men associate even today with the name and genius of Hippocrates. Here is its form as it has endured through all the changing centuries: "You shall diligently inquire, and true presentment make, of all such matters and things as shall be given you in charge; the counsel of the people of this state, your fellows' and your own you shall keep secret; you shall present no person from envy, hatred and malice; nor shall you leave any one unpresented through fear, favor, affection or reward, or hope thereof; but you shall present all things truly as they come to your knowledge, according to the best of your understanding. So help you God!"

Like the tones of a mighty bell, these echoing notes of adjuration bring back our straying thoughts to sanctity and service. I cannot listen to them without a thrill. Here, I say to myself, here indeed, secreted in this solemn formula, is the true spirit of the law which knows no fear nor favor. Not all her ministers have been true to the ideal which she has held aloft for them to follow. But here, imperishably preserved amid the grime and dust of centuries, the word has been proclaimed, to steady us when we seem to falter, to strengthen us when we seem to weaken, to tell us that with all the failings and backslidings, with all the fears and all the prejudice, the spirit is still pure.

And so it still is for the great profession that is mine, as still it is for yours, which year by year renews in conduct and in speech the pledge and promise of Hippocrates.

I thank you for the privilege that has been given me of bringing the two together in this hall of your Academy.

THE AMERICAN LAW INSTITUTE[1]

THE existence of this Institute is a declaration to the world that "laissez faire" in law is going or has gone the way of "laissez faire" in economics.

A gospel of effort takes the place of a gospel that has vacillated between inaction and despair. We will not sit by and refuse to do anything because the voice of pessimism may remind us with labored demonstration that try as hard as we may, we shall be unable to do everything. The changing mood reveals a changing outlook upon law, and the processes and methods that develop and perfect it. Throw yourself back, they used to tell us, upon the broad currents of history, and let the tide of the centuries sweep you to your goal. This

[1] The American Law Institute, organized at Washington in February, 1923, has set before itself the task of preparing a restatement of the principles of the common law.

This address was made at the Third Annual Meeting, May 1, 1925.

was comforting doctrine, and doctrine that the inertia native to most of us made it pleasurable to follow, if only tide and current could be trusted to do their share. The wisdom of the precept was not doubted till we found ourselves sinking when the program required us to be floating, and doubt deepened into certainty upon the discovery that instead of moving to a haven, we were sprawling on the rocks. In one of these moments of discomfiture, this Institute was formed.

The year that has gone by since our last meeting has brought steady and substantial progress achieved by unremitting labor. I shall make no attempt to put before you in this address the details of our activities or to cover their entire range. You will find a fuller narrative in the report of our Director, to whose tact and wisdom and self-sacrificing industry the members of the Institute owe a debt, not easily computed, for whatever of bright promise attends their enterprise today. My concern at the moment is with the larger aspects of the problem. Again, as at our last meeting, a tribute is due to the spirit in which the Reporters, their advisers and assistants have approached the task before them. They have exhibited a patience and devotion that would be impossible were it not for the sustaining power of a belief that something monumental and enduring is taking shape under their hands. Draft after draft has been submitted and corrected, only to give way in the end to some new objection, entailing revision yet again, till minds less trained to scientific inquiry or less moved by its disinterested spirit, would have petulantly resigned the task, or challenged carping criticism to offer something better. One finds it hard to exaggerate the difficulties that have been met and overborne. They become manifest as soon as we attempt to reproduce in thought the steps and stages of the project. At the beginning there has been need to gather from the pronouncements of the courts the principle or the rule implicit in their judgments, to find the soul of the decision beneath its integument of clay. This in itself is a wearisome and poignant task, especially when the soul reveals itself in the end as a soul already lost, an erring and blighted spirit, unworthy to be released, lest, meeting its fellow spirits, it poison and corrupt them. But this is only part of the travail and the agony. You choose after long debate the principle or the rule that you are ready to espouse, and you think you understand it. There lies before you still the task of expressing it in words. At once new vistas of uncertainty are opened to your gaze. It is hard enough, shunning generalities, or putting them forward timidly as merely approximate hypotheses, to declare the rights and wrongs engendered by a concrete situation, definitely envisaged. It is harder still when, abandoning particulars, we must announce in magisterial tones the rationalizing principle in which particulars are enveloped, the coördinating rule under which they are subsumed.

This is the high emprise on which the scholars of the Institute have ventured. Not for them those provisional and tentative formulas, those reservations and conditions, those shadings and softenings, by which judges, made wary by many an ambush, have saved for hours of extremity an avenue of retreat. By the form and method chosen, the framers of the restatement have courted danger and defied it. In the fierce light that beats upon these categorical propositions, standing stark and unprotected in the open, there is room for truth and for error, but seldom for half truth or truth unwilling to declare itself. By all this the difficulty of the process is multiplied many fold, and multiplied the danger. I do not say that the authors of the restatement have triumphed over these obstacles altogether, that they have found it possible to handle universals as freely and securely as their brethren on the bench have been dealing with particulars. Only powers superhuman could compass that achievement. Indeed, I have ventured to believe that if the general scheme or spirit of their work was to be criticized at all, at least in some of the preliminary drafts, it was in a certain search and seeking now and again for definiteness and assurance and finality in fields where definiteness and assurance and finality must be left to the agency of time. Even that criticism is little applicable to the restatements now before you. It points, however, to a danger that we must be vigilant to avert. You will acquit me, I hope, of a merely selfish desire to exalt the prestige or the power of my guild if I say that in determining the tendencies and directions of legal development in the future, something will have to be left, even when the restatement is completed, to those tentative gropings, those cautious experiments, those provisional hypotheses, that are part of the judicial process. No group of men can be expected to be invariably at one in the location of the line of division between one method and the other, between impressionism and dogma. None the less, if we take it by and large, the outcome of the redactions is an admirable compromise and a memorable achievement. Many of the rules and principles to be extracted from the enormous body of our case law are there in the opinions, not as precepts explicitly avowed, but as assumptions, presuppositions, things felt rather than perceived. We may say the same thing of most of our legal treatises, for, in them as in judicial opinions, the discursive method of exposition does not lend itself readily to precision and completeness. Now, almost for the first time, at least on any scale so large, a multitude of these rules and principles, gathered from their setting and scientifically arranged, have been stated tersely, accurately, fully, with a definiteness of form approaching the pronouncements of a statute. We are now to see whether our law has found a medium of expression that will solve or help to solve the age-long problem of uniting flexibility to certainty, that will give us the virtues of a code without the blighting pretension to literal inerrancy, a code that instead of repressing the forces and tendencies of growth by the imposition upon the law of a form forever fixed, will stir them to new life by its revelation of a harmony and an order till then unthought of and unseen.

Today we lay before you the first fruits of the harvest. Much more has been done than these offerings might lead you to believe. Drafts of many other sections have been written and rewritten. We bring to you those sections only that have reached some measure of finality. The subject of Conflict of Laws is represented by forty-two sections, covering the law of domicile. If we were to put before you all the sections that have been covered by preliminary drafts, we could show you 156 sections of restatement and commentary covering jurisdiction in its general principles, and then, in greater detail, executive jurisdiction, legislative jurisdiction, and finally judicial jurisdiction, which has proved the most troublesome of all. To this there should be added seventy-nine sections dealing with the jurisdiction of a state to tax, which we have determined to discard as not falling within the scope of this restatement, though we hope to utilize it hereafter when the time arrives for a restatement of the law governing taxation. The subject of the law of Contracts is represented by seventy-two sections, dealing with fundamental definitions, the general principles governing the formation of contracts, and more particularly those governing the formation of the contracts classified as informal. Progress has been made, however, in the preparation of more than 100 other sections, dealing with such subjects as the formation of formal contracts, joint contractual rights and obligations, contractual rights of persons not parties to the contract, the assignment of rights and the delegation of duties. The subject of the law of torts is represented by seventy-seven sections dealing with some of the fundamental rights of personality. Progress has been made in the preparation of many more sections dealing in part with other rights of personality and in part with rights of property. The subject of Agency having been taken up later than the other subjects, is not before you at all, but the Reporter and his advisers are already well advanced in the preparation of 119 sections which deal with fundamental problems. Besides all this, we have a report by Dr. Lewis, covering the classification of Business Associations and indicating his own views as to the clearest and most fruitful treatment of the topic. If your appetites are not satisfied by what is set before you now, we can promise you a year hence a banquet so abundant that none of you will be permitted to go unsated from the feast. The dainties and tidbits of the law will be served in such profusion as to make the tables groan, to say nothing of the members. Sufficient, however, for the day are its labors and perplexities.

I warn you at the outset that they are neither few nor trivial. The subject the most innocent on the surface may turn out when it is probed to be charged with hidden fire. We begin with the Conflict of Laws, and surprise awaits us at the threshold. Domicile suggests the home, with the peace, the freedom from contention, that is thought to reign about the fireside. If you had been present at our conferences, you would feel with me that strife, though it be excluded from the sanctuary, is hovering close at hand. I know my own home, and am prepared, even after following the restatement, to maintain its identity against the competition of localities less favored. I am not so ready as once I might have been, to make unqualified assertions about the moorings of my friends. Perhaps you will think, since it is all a matter of definition, that the difference is not so very important after all, and that we are making a lot of fuss and pother about niceties of nomenclature. This is where I have an unfair advantage of you, for I have seen the later installments, and I know the dénouement of the story. I find as the plot thickens that the definition with which we start, far from being a matter of merely curious or speculative interest, makes all the difference in the world in determining the rule with which we end. Make no mistake. This narrow distinction between domicile and residence may start you in life as an heir or a pauper, and later, when you have grown up, may marry or divorce you. We must keep a close watch on its pretensions, and the time to watch is now. There is a lesson to be drawn from all this, for it is not for the mere humor of the thing that I have ventured to bring it to your notice. The lesson is, indeed, twofold, and the more our restatement progresses, the more we shall be conscious of its significance, and that in both its phases. There is a lesson for legal science and a lesson for legal philosophy. The lesson for legal science is that the structure depends on the foundations; that the fundamental conceptions of the law breed others in their image, and that the progeny will be misshapen or distorted, unless the parent conceptions are sound and pure and clear, as only accurate analysis can make us certain that they are. But there is still another lesson, and this a lesson for legal philosophy or rather perhaps a warning. If fundamental conceptions are capable of this propagating power, at what point shall they be checked? Shall we follow their implications down the line as long as we can trace them to the limit of their logic? When, if at all, shall they yield to other and competing forces, the forces, let us say, of utility or convenience or usage or justice or mere luxuriant diversity? I shall not develop this inquiry by pointing out its practical application. I shall do no more than whet your appetite for the later numbers of the serial by promising you that such inquiries will be found to be very pertinent when you come to deal with some of the problems of judicial jurisdiction. I have felt so keenly about some of them that at one or two conferences I have had the temerity to break a lance in debate with Prof. Beale, knowing that it could be only honor and no disgrace to be unhorsed by such a foeman. Perhaps we are beginning to see that our differences will turn out in the end to be largely a war of words, and that by a few verbal emendations, logic and justice and convenience, which seemed to be far apart, may be brought together and reconciled and made to live in amity. I suspect that this is only typical of what has often happened before in other branches of the law, and that many a bizarre and harsh conclusion, supposed to be the legitimate offspring of a conception or a formula, will be shown forth as bastard when the formula or conception is recast in truer mold. So it is that the methods by which law develops, supply checks on one another, justice and utility putting us on the scent, so to speak, to discover and unearth what is spurious in logic. But the interesting thing, after all, is not the settlement of this little controversy or that, the adoption of one rule or another in some narrow and restricted field. The interesting thing is to find that the fabric which comes off the loom of the law, like the fabric of life itself, is all of a single piece; that you can hardly mar or mend it at one point without marring or mending at others; and that seams and scars persist, and splendors and glories too, long after the moving shuttle has left them far behind.

I turn to the law of torts, and I find stuff for comment there. The installment before you deals with some of the rights of personality. If we were following the traditional arrangement, we should say that the subjects treated are battery, assault, and false imprisonment. Not the least of the merits of Prof. Bohlen's work is his departure from the traditional arrangement with its basis in the forms of actions, and his adoption of another dependent upon the nature of the interest invaded or the right infringed. The old arrangement did much, I think, to choke and stunt the law of torts in its natural and free development, its development in harmony with changing human needs. The tendency was for rights and duties to relate themselves to procedural restrictions instead of narrowing and broadening in correspondence with the human interests that are worthy of protection. I think the value of the new approach will be increasingly manifest when the later installments of the work shall introduce us to problems even more complex. For the moment, however, I am concerned with the present installment and no others. Here again, as in the Conflict of Laws, I gain a vivid sense of the vast accumulation of acquired and modifying characteristics that a legal conception, in its origin apparently the most simple, absorbs and gathers to itself in its march through the centuries with an expanding legal system. When I heard that the subjects to be covered at the beginning were battery, assault and false imprisonment, I thought there would be easy travel. I ask you to take my word for it, we have met with hard roads, and worse passes are ahead. A blow in the face seems a fairly palpable fact, but all sorts of mental reservations and concomitants have to be known and estimated before you can determine whether it is to be reckoned as an actionable wrong. The psychical is ever crowding upon the precincts of the physical. Was the blow an unprovoked affront? Was it in defense of life or property? Was it struck with leave and license? Can leave and license justify, or is there some public policy that overrides consent? Even our bodily persons may receive a fictitious extension, so to speak, by identification with the things that are closely attached to them, whether by physical bonds or by the invisible ligaments of thought and spirit. If these and like problems arise when we deal with acts and injuries that must have agitated the cavemen, we gain some notion of the troubles to come later when forgetting primitive man, we shall have to deal with wrongs that have their origin in a complex order of society—oppressive combinations, malicious interference with another's opportunities for betterment, the thousand and one devices of hatred, greed and envy.

I am not sure how to formulate the lesson that these difficulties teach, the warning that they give. Perhaps their precept is the same as the benison that has come to us from ancient days: Be bold. Be ever bold. Be not too bold. It is but a human impulse if the framers of a restatement are tempted to declare the law not only as the past has shaped it in judgments already rendered, but as the future ought to shape it in cases yet to come. Those of us whose lives have been spent on the bench or at the bar have learned caution and reticence, perhaps even in excess. We know the value of the veiled phrase, the blurred edge, the uncertain line. Well, I am strong for them even now, at least in their proper places, or rather, I ought to say, for reservations and limitations which will preserve whatever of value there may be in impressionistic forms and phrases. Undoubtedly, much may be done in the treatises supporting the restatements, with their more discursive methods, to mark the tendencies and directions that will determine growth hereafter. I am speaking of the magisterial pronouncements of the restatements themselves. In these, let us give definiteness and fixity of outline where there is definiteness and fixity in the law as it exists or where argument so preponderates that a choice is fairly safe. Let us not hesitate, however, in other situations to say in all frankness that the problem is yet unsolved, and while indicating competing considerations either way, to leave the answer to the years.

I have no time to remind you of the interesting problems in the law of Contracts that are latent in the preliminary chapters already in your hands. The choice between the objective and the subjective conception of a contract with all that this implies will have been made when these sections go forth with the *imprimatur* of the Institute. There is, however, one other problem that I am anxious to bring to your attention before the installments and the treatises accompanying them are made the subjects of discussion. So far as the restatements themselves are concerned, we have worked out during the two years of our existence a form and a method and a technique which, at least in their fundamental features, are not likely to be changed. It is otherwise, however, with the treatises. These have been put together with some haste, at least comparatively speaking, in order to give some understanding of the authorities and considerations supporting our conclusions. You will find, however, not only that they differ among themselves, but that still other forms are possible, and it is for the Council and the members to indicate their preference, if preference there be. Shall the treatise be encyclopedic in its scope, collating all the pertinent authorities, a complete exposition of the law in the present stage of its development? Shall it follow a method more selective, choosing typical cases, not meagerly, indeed, and yet not with indiscriminate profusion—so many as will illustrate and justify the principles and rules of the restatement, or exhibit the conflict of authorities—a balanced and orderly commentary, the distilled essence and elixir of study and reflection? Or finally discarding these forms, shall the treatise take the shape of notes upon doubtful or contentious passages, leaving others, neither uncertain nor disputed, to be verified by other means? I have my own notion as to the method that is preferable, though it is easier to express a preference than to draft the treatise that will give to an idea the reality of performance. Perhaps in the end we shall settle down to one method as the true one. Perhaps we shall find, on the other hand, that there must be a diversity of methods, as the nature of the subject emphasizes the need of expansion or compression. I am hopeful that your deliberations will yield suggestion and enlightenment that will clarify the choice.

My final word must be one of hope and grateful recognition. We may not accomplish all that we have planned. It is yet too soon to say. At least, there has been a brave beginning.

Swift in his *Tale of a Tub* made the father give to each of three sons a legacy of a new coat. "You are to understand," said the father, "that these coats have two virtues contained in them: one is that with good wearing they will last you fresh and sound as long as you live; the other is that they will grow in the same proportion as your bodies, lengthening and widening of themselves, so as to be always fit." The common law, it seems, is one of these coats, or so at least we have treated it. The body that it was meant to shield has grown; and we have been brought up in the faith that the coat would grow too. So, indeed, it seems to have done, for its stuff is as elastic as any that is made. Even now with all the wear and tear, it is still a good coat, far too good to be thrown away, though the stretching and the shrinking have not been uniform throughout, so that the sleeves are perhaps a little too short, and the tails, which are useless and old-fashioned anyhow, a trifle too long. Let us make it over as reverently as our fathers made it for us, and hand it down to our descendants.

THE HOME OF THE LAW[1]

Brethren of the Bench and Bar:

To the cause to which our lives are dedicate, we now dedicate a home.

No temple this, with majesty of arch and pillar, with fretted vault and dim and awesome spaces. The genius of the spirit that will dwell within these walls is one too intimate, too friendly, too human, to be symbolized in forms designed for reverence and worship. And yet, no factory this, no mere coöperative office building, no bourse for sordid money getting, no mart of trade and commerce. The indwelling spirit will not be coaxed within these walls—will not irradiate their stones with the benediction of her presence—unless something finer than mere gain is here to beckon and beguile her. All this our architect has

[1] Address at the dedication of the new home of the New York County Lawyers' Association, May 26, 1930.

seen, and made visible to the eye of sense in forms of truth and beauty. He has chosen his symbol wisely. Not the symbol of the temple, still less the symbol of the market, but one gentler, simpler, friendlier, more intimate in its suggestions, more universal in its appeal, the symbol of the home.

So in this colonial dwelling, built in a style that Washington knew, facing the church in which Washington worshiped, this great family of the Bar of New York comes together today to renew the old greetings of brotherly devotion, to feel the uplift that is born of community of effort, and to make high resolve that never shall the indwelling spirit have cause to turn her face away for any stain of wrong to the honor of the family.

Why has this structure taken shape through the contributions of a few for the satisfaction of the many? What has kindled the generous ardor that has found expression in these forms? Not the mere desire to lay the foundations of a library to which students may repair. There are law institutes and reading rooms already, and new ones could be built at a fraction of this cost, if what was sought were nothing more. Not the will to create a club-house, a mere place of recreation. If play were the sole aim, there would be competitors too many and too strenuous on hill and dale and stream. If you would know the soul of our building, you must seek for something more than these. Library and club and meeting-house indeed are here, but neither singly nor collectively do they give the key to the structure, the secret of its life. I do not mean that its planners have been indifferent to mere convenience. Why, I am credibly informed that there is to be a pent-house on the roof where the pent-up emotions of the bar may find appropriate release when strained beyond endurance by the stupidity of judges. A worthy end again; yet even that, I am convinced, is not the key to the ardor that animates these stones. I go back to my Plato, as so many wiser than I have gone throughout the years, and in one of his eternal questions, I seem to see prefigured the answer to my own. "Can virtue then be taught?" The words are those of Dr. Woodbridge in a summary of Plato's thought.

"Can virtue then be taught? Can education make a man good? The question is asked again and again in Plato's pages, but never receives a straight-forward unequivocal answer. It is left a question, the insistent human question as we make our way through the changes and chances of this mortal life."

Well, education means many things, and a building like this is one of our modern answers to Plato's deathless query. There is education in books, but education in life also; education in solitude, but education also in the crowd; education in study, but education even greater in the contagion of example. Ask any youth who has gone through a university what part of his training has counted most in later life. Almost invariably, I am sure, the first place will be given, not to shreds of information, the book-learning of the schools, but to the transfigured sense of values that is born of companionship with lofty minds, the living and the dead. There is more to be bestowed by Alma Mater than the possession of a sheep-skin. There is more in membership in the bar than a license to sign a brief or intone a prosy argument.

This home has been built and is now opened in that faith. It has been built and is now opened in the faith that this great conglomerate bar of ours, sodden and inert at times by reason of that very weight which might make it so irresistible a power for good, will yet be stirred in all its depths by the ferment of high thoughts and fine ideals, if once the leaven of fraternity shall vitalize the mass. Here in this home it will be given to us all to feel ourselves a part of an immemorial succession, to feel the pride and the poetry of keeping the succession true, and the shame and the taunt when it is ravished and disgraced. Who will forfeit the privilege of crossing the threshold of the dwelling house, an equal among equals? Who will deface and deflower the family inheritance when once he feels it to be *his* inheritance—when he counts as his own the memories and traditions that seem even as I speak, to be taking on a new form, to have become visible and incarnate in this hall resplendent with their presence?

There is in the making here a new and heightened sense of kinship that will bind us together with a tie of family solidarity, closer and more permanent than any that can be known without a common home, a common gathering place, a common focus and center of family activities. Here will develop the sense of corporate responsibility that will cause us all to tingle as at a personal affront when the honor of the guild is assailed in literature or in life with words of cynical disdain. Take this for illustration from the correspondence of Disraeli, his famous letter to Charles Austin, who had charged him with an attempt to bribe the voters at an election. "I am informed," he wrote, "that it is quite useless and even unreasonable in me to expect from Mr. Austin any satisfaction for those impertinent calumnies, because Mr. Austin is a member of an honorable profession, the first principle of whose practice appears to be that they may say anything provided they be paid for it. The principle of circulating falsehoods with impunity is delicately described as doing your duty towards your client, which appears to be a very different process from doing your duty towards your neighbor."

How the studied insolence of this thrust has kept its edge through all the years! How the flesh recoils and quivers even now as the words come hissing to the ear! One wonders how many of the men and women of our own day can hear in these reverberating taunts an echo of their own beliefs. One wonders how many have found fuel for such beliefs and worse in the scandals of the day and hour. One wonders how many are judging us, not by our best, but by our worst, and are visiting upon one and all the scorn and condemnation that should be the portion of a few. Here and now in the opening of the new building, the consecration of the home, let there be a rebirth of the resolve to smother such reproaches by lives that will render them impossible, and to prove ourselves worthy of our heritage of opportunity and power.

I have spoken of our heritage, and what a heritage it is! How many-sided in its interests! How rich in anecdote and story! Nothing in the whole realm of knowledge but is grist for our mill. The truth is brought home to one at times in unexpected turns and corners. I like to go through the old books and see how many of the ways of lawyers —habits and mannerisms to appearance the most modern—have their roots in distant centuries. We reproduce the ways of our predecessors as children and grandchildren recall the gait and manners of their ancestors. In the days of ancient Greece, the litigants recited speeches that were drafted for them by professional orators who were eloquent for a price. If you will turn to Dobson on *The Greek Orators*, you will find that a litigant hard beset would dwell with humility upon his own meager powers of eloquence or persuasion, and beseech the jurors to be on their guard against the eloquence and persuasion of his more experienced and gifted adversary. Why, you can go into the City Court of New York any day of the term, unless things have greatly changed since I used to practice law, and hear the same argument from men who would stare at you in wonderment if you were to tell them it was Attic Greek. Only the other day I was reading in convenient translation a speech by Cicero, extolled by rhetoricians, the oration in behalf of Archias, and the sly old advocate worked in page after page of wholly irrelevant digression in the belief that it would help if only he could create an atmosphere in favor of his client. He did it without being called to account and reminded of the issue, just as sometimes even now a perfervid orator will work in like digressions without being held to the point by the master of the revels, if so, without disrespect, I may characterize the judge presiding on the bench. There is nothing new in such frailties, the last infirmities of noble minds. Still less is there anything new in the ineradicable tendency of the guilty, or even of the innocent, to divert the issue from themselves and direct it to the conduct and motives and reputation of the complainant, the source of all the trouble. You can see the impulse exemplified in orations the most famous. Demosthenes in his oration on the Crown roundly vilified the prosecutor, who had all the evil qualities, it seems, that have been inherited by district attorneys in the view at least of counsel who practice in the court of sessions. Inveterate, too, has been the habit of inordinate prolixity. From time immemorial judges have struggled fruitlessly against it, offering rewards to brevity and laying burdens on garrulity, but all to small avail. Some one gave me only recently an order by the Court of Chancery made three centuries ago in which the draftsman of a verbose and impertinent replication was ordered to walk about the court with the pleading hanging about his neck and pay a fine to boot. Our methods of repression are less rigorous today, but the chancery replication was probably a *feuilleton*, an innocent brochure, when compared with briefs that I could offer as exhibits if the angry chancellor were here. In my own court, as you know, the time allowed for the argument of an appeal from a judgment used to be two hours on each side. Luckily comparatively few lawyers took advantage of the privilege, due, I think, to a pretty general notion that with us, as in the Appellate Division, the limit was an hour. Recently we have amended our rule to make it more in harmony with the current misconception. I understand that in other states, for example Pennsylvania, the time is even shorter, and that neither the court nor the cause of justice has suffered from the change, though I am not advised to what extent the clipping of the wings of flight has brought suffering to counsel. My heart smites me at times at the thought of curbing them at all. After all, there is something captivating in their zeal, something human and lovable, even if a little wearing. If they wander from the point, they never do so quite so blatantly as Demosthenes or Cicero.

When I meditate upon these things, the enthusiasms of forensic efforts, the fire that goes into them, the meaning of defeat or victory, not merely to the pocket of the advocate, but still more to his pride, his repute and his sense of duty done, I think with mounting wonder of the spirit of fraternal fellowship that animates the profession even now—the good temper, the humor, the acceptance of fortune fair or foul as all in the day's work. Especially I am impressed with the kindness and generosity of the bar in its relations to the bench. "We take our pleasures sadly," says an English essayist, writing of his countrymen, "but we take our troubles with a smile." Perhaps that is not a bad summary of the spirit of the bar. We judges are doing things all the time that must disappoint you sorely. We are handing down decisions in closely balanced cases where the patient and careful work, for months and even years, of conscientious members of the bar is shattered overnight. If one were to consider such a situation in the abstract, without knowledge of the facts, one might suppose that the result would be a chronic state of irritation and hostility between two contending camps. Nothing of the kind! If we do the day's work with a reasonable measure of intelligence and devotion, we are rewarded by a friendship which is really more than friendship—by a friendship so tinged with emotion that we can only describe it as affection. I can speak for one judge at least in saying that it evokes in his heart an affectionate response.

Popular the members of our profession have never been able to become through all the ages of its history. Perhaps that is one of the reasons why they have clung to one another with the solidarity that everywhere is born of persecution or resistance. It is a feature of nearly every Utopia, from Plato down to H. G. Wells, that there has been no place in it for lawyers. Here in the new world, the ancient hostility had certainly not vanished in colonial days and later. You will find it all commemorated very soon in that museum of our colonial legal history which was promised you today, the latest benefaction of the Maecenas of our bar. Hostility was not left to dubious or halting inference. I ran across the following a while ago, in rereading Lowell's letters. It is an extract from *The Letters of an American Farmer*, written in 1782. "Lawyers," he writes, "are plants that will grow in any soil that is cultivated by the hand of others, and when once they have taken root, they will extinguish every vegetable that grows around them. . . . The most ignorant, the most bungling member of that profession will, if placed in the most obscure part of the country, promote litigiousness, and amass more wealth without labor than the most opulent farmer with all his toils. . . . What a pity that our forefathers, who happily extinguished so many fatal customs, and expunged from their new government so many errors and abuses, both religious and civil, did not also prevent the introduction of a set of men so dangerous." Already, about a century before, Georgia had acted on this or like advice, and attempted to rid herself of the pest. She passed a single ordinance for the prohibition of rum and lawyers. She let up afterwards upon the less flagrant of these evils, but she was inexorable about the lawyers. In New York, however, there were troubles of a different kind. Here, marvelous to relate, the lawyers were too few. In 1695 there were only forty-one lawyers in New York, and litigants with money used to retain the whole bar of the locality, leaving no one for their adversaries. Accordingly in the same year an act was adopted by the assembly of the Province to regulate the number of lawyers that any litigant might retain, just as laws were enacted to regulate the enjoyment of other luxuries of life. The number was fixed at two. "If they retain any more," said the statute, "it shall be lawful for the justices of the Bench where the suit is depending to order all such attorneys as shall be retained, more than two as aforesaid, to plead for the other side, without returning the fee received, anything contained in this or any other act to the contrary hereof in any wise notwithstanding." There was poetic justice for you! Lawyer number 3 or lawyer number 4, retained and paid by an enthusiastic plaintiff, might turn up on the day of the trial, the money in his pocket, espousing the cause of the defendant. What would our Grievance Committees have to say about such practices today? I must admit that in my judgment it would have been fairer, if every client was to be limited to two lawyers, to provide that every lawyer should be furnished with two clients. Very likely such a guaranty is a blessing too great to be attainable in any earthly commonwealth. At any rate the lawyers seem to have worried along without it. I wish the draftsmen of the act of 1695 could have a look at us today.

Evolutionists will have to tell us whether some vestigial survival of the spirit of these old colonial days when we were a little band of forty abides with us even now. The fashion is in these times to dwell upon the shortcomings of the bar and to touch lightly on its virtues. None the less, with all its faults and failings, it has exhibited in the main a comradeship, a spirit of good fellowship, which owes something of its persistence perhaps to the traditions of the inns of court, but which is seen to be something distinctive when we contrast it with the envies and suspicions in callings more or less allied. Shakespeare has told us in the lines so often quoted that we are to do "as adversaries do at law, strive mightily, but eat and drink as friends." The picture and the practice are so familiar that we have come to take for granted the spirit they exhibit. But it is not so commonplace as it seems. Asquith in his *Memories and Reflections* reminds us that among the leaders of the House of Commons there have been conflicting views as to the propriety of statesmen's holding friendly personal relations with their political opponents. So sturdy a figure as John Bright announced his opposition to the practice with constancy and vehemence. The seductions of a dinner were thought to have a tendency to mollify convictions and stimulate with the gastric juices a tendency to compromise. The tendency may be admitted, but, nowadays at least, men are seldom sure enough of their convictions to be willing to put inflexibility in the forefront of the virtues and compromise behind it. For lawyers, at all events, there has been a different tradition in England as with us. Perhaps the reason is that our rôles as champions for contending litigants are cut out for us in advance upon lines determinate and known. There is less of the dim penumbra, the borderland of vague approach, in which the views of the protagonists of the political arena shade off by insensible gradations from conformity into difference. For us, in any event, the tradition of fellowship and comradeship is something very fine and precious, to be stimulated and nourished with vivid recognition of its fructifying value. I can think of nothing more likely to foster it, to bring its seeds to maturity and reap the benefit of its fruits, than the building of a home wherein lawyers of all conditions, the old and the young, the great and the humble, may come together as co-workers and as equals in the spirit of the great democracy of justice in whose name they have enrolled.

We praise and celebrate today the symmetry of walls. Within those walls, in days now far away, when all our voices shall be hushed, an unnumbered multitude of our brethren will be busy with the endless quest for a symmetry still greater, the symmetry that men call justice, the adaptation of the rule of life to the symmetry they call divine.

May the work be worthy of the monument; the workers, of the home.

THE GAME OF THE LAW AND ITS PRIZES[1]

Members of the Graduating Class, Ladies and Gentlemen:

SIR FREDERICK POLLOCK tells us in his new *Essays in the Law* that in medieval times there was a special patron saint to whom students used to pray that they might pass their examinations. The records do not inform us, he says, whether the intercession of the saint was supposed to strengthen the brain of the students, or soften the heart of the examiner. Enough that her power, whether exerted one way or the other, was never doubted by the faithful.

I remember the sense of relief, of an incubus cast aside, with which I took my last examination after the years that I had passed in college and in law school. There, I said to myself, was a chapter closed. I might make mistakes in the future, but I

[1] Address at the seventy-fourth commencement of the Albany Law School, June 10, 1925.

should no longer make them under the eye of examiners charged with the special duty of exposing my failings and giving them a quantitative value in comparison with my virtues. Exposure thereafter would be, so to speak, a matter of chance. A class of professional detectives would be no longer on my tracks.

I suppose some such dreams of felicity are stirring and elating you tonight. It gives me pain to dispel them, yet dreams they are, and nothing more. As long as you live, and surely as long as you practice law, an examiner will dog your footsteps. When you enter some law office, an apprentice to some older lawyer, there will be some one looking over your shoulder, criticizing your work, pointing out its defects, cheering you, once in a while, by a concession of its merits, educating, examining, testing—the process repeated without end. When a little later you start for yourselves, there will be trial judges and juries and appellate courts, all examining, testing, approving or rejecting, just as in the days of adolescence which you thought were left behind. Sometimes when these critics are compassionate or silent, you will have to meet a test still sterner, a scrutiny yet more rigid, the merciless test and scrutiny of a defeated and reproachful client. As years go by, some of you may cease to be advocates, and gain a seat upon the Bench. You may think then that you are safe, but alas! it is not so. Examiners still crowd about, and no longer are they to be propitiated by the invocation of a patron saint. If you happen to be a trial judge, there are the judges of the appellate courts. If you mount to one of those courts yourself, there are your colleagues, ever lying in ambush, vigilant and keen, and perhaps some other court yet higher than your own. If you live through all these dangers with reason unimpaired, there are other trials as searching. The Bar, with its associations and committees, and, worse than these, the law schools and the law reviews, are still waiting at the door. Let there be a joint in your armor, a flaw in your opinion, it will not be long before probe and scalpel will expose a gaping wound. The examiner is near at hand.

So, in very truth, gentlemen, this is not the end

at all, but only the commencement. I was reading a few weeks ago a book by Abraham Flexner on *Medical Education* which has a lesson for lawyers too. "As a matter of fact," he says, "schools of engineering do not produce engineers or architects; schools of law do not produce lawyers. The school's part is largely limited to training in method and technique, and to inspiration." Method is much, technique is much, but inspiration is even more. If you go out into the world thinking that the ordeal is over, or that it will be over when you have leapt one hurdle yet to come, the hurdle maintained by the State Board of Law Examiners, not very far away, if you go out into the world in this spirit, there will be the shock of many a disillusionment before the course is run. But if you bear in mind the truth that this is only the commencement, that troubles are only beginning, and if you act upon that faith, behold, by some subtle necromancy, the pain that you foresee shall be transmuted into joy. The troubles will emerge as triumphs; the travail and the doubt will yield an unexpected peace; the great truth will have been learned that the quest is greater than what is sought, the effort finer than the prize, or, rather, that the effort *is* the prize—the victory cheap and hollow were it not for the rigor of the game.

I have spoken of it as a "game" and so indeed it is, though it will depend upon your notion of a game whether the metaphor shall elevate or cheapen. It is a game, but it is a game of skill, and that is why there has been need of this elaborate preparation to give you a working knowledge of its rules, of its method and technique. When I contrast the training that is given to the law student of today with the training that was given to me in the prehistoric days before my admission to the bar, I am filled with a spirit of envy that makes me anxious to step down and take my place in your ranks, forgetting, for the moment, that your examiners would probably refuse to pass me. In the days of my study at the law school, we had courses in the law of contracts, real estate, torts, equity, evidence, and practice. That was about all, and this little was taught out of some old-fashioned textbook, with slight reference to the cases and little or no discussion of them by students or professors. Take such a subject as the law of corporations; we had no instruction in it at all. Perhaps the notion was that no corporation would be foolish enough to retain us at the beginning, and that by the time such retainers came to us we could pick up the knowledge for ourselves. Whatever may have been the reason, I do no more than report the fact. If some one had asked us to state the difference between a bond and a share of stock, I fear that most of us, for all that we had learned to the contrary at law school, would have been in the position of a woman of my acquaintance, who, when a similar question was propounded to her, eyed her questioner quizzically for a moment, and then exclaimed triumphantly, "I know. They are the same." So it is that in an envious spirit I contrast my own meager preparation with the copious and varied courses that it has been your privilege to follow.

You have gained something, however, which is more than mere knowledge of principles and rules and precedents. These are so many and so diverse that with all the facilities of the modern law school and with all the industry and zeal that you could exhibit in the endeavor to become masters of them, you would find in the end that you had only scratched the surface. The thing even more important that you have learned is the ability to think legally, an understanding of the method, the technique, by which the judicial process works. It is in truth a fascinating process, baffling, elusive, infinite in the variety of its aspects, and yet infinite also in its appeal to the heart and mind and spirit of generous and ambitious youth. The new generations bring with them their new problems which call for new rules, to be patterned, indeed, after the rules of the past, and yet adapted to the needs and the justice of another day and hour. Yours will be the task of formulating these rules when we, who have done our little as best we could, shall have laid the burden down. One must be historian and prophet all in one—the qualities of each united in a perfect blend—who would fulfill that task completely. Rights and duties are to be defined in such terms as to fit them to the complexities of modern life, yet all the time, in defining them, we speak the words and perpetuate the thought of the judges of long ago who penned some ancient writ of emperor or king. "The last of the Caesars has fallen," I quote the words of Roscoe Pound, "but the thought of the jurisconsults of the days of the first Caesar is still law in half of the world." Here is a game, a puzzle, a conundrum, to mystify and pique. Here is a task, a summons, a vocation, to rouse and stir and quicken. Give what you have, whether what you have be much or little. You will be sharers in a process that is greater than the greatest of its ministers.

Yes, indeed, it is a wonderful and inspiring opportunity that confronts you in this year of grace as you turn your backs upon the law school to take your places at the bar. The process of justice is never finished, but reproduces itself, generation after generation, in ever-changing forms, and today, as in the past, it calls for the bravest and the best. Pretty soon we old fellows shall be leaving the scene, and you will be coming forward to fill the broken ranks. I should like to come back a generation or so from now, just to get a peep at the state of the law, make my bow, and retire. I suppose I should find big changes. Many of the opinions that I have written would probably by that time have been overruled, or charitably distinguished. The chief effort of my successors would be, very likely, to find some respectful and respectable way of avoiding or forgetting them. These things might distress me a little, but I have small doubt they would be right. I should feel, doubtless, when I thought it all over, that the movement was in the right direction, that we were getting closer to the goal. Very possibly I should wish to know the names of those who were doing the work of the day, who were carrying the standard forward, who were keeping alive the great tradition. They would show me the roll of honor, and there I should read the names of some who look into my face tonight. It will be your fault if it is not so.

I come back to my metaphor of a game, a game

which exacts skill, but which, like every game worth playing, exacts something more important, and that something is the sportsman's spirit, which is only another word for character. This is the chief thing, more important far than skill, for skill without this will be palsied and perverted. Play the game like sportsmen, or give it up at the beginning, and choose some other calling, which, if its aims are less exalted, will at least spare you the reproach of insincerity, since its members will not have pledged themselves to be votaries of justice. I do not ask the impossible. I know that for most of you, the law, though a profession, must also be a means of livelihood. I know that worldly success is pleasant in itself, and that it is also for many who live in the world the badge of all success. I do not ask you to turn yourselves into hypocrites by pretending that you are indifferent to it, or that you would not gain it and gain it in the fullest measure if you could have it on terms consistent with dignity and honor. But you would not cheat at football or at tennis or at cards, though the game were thereby assured to you and detection a remote possibility, or even impossible altogether. You would know that your honor had been pledged, and the zest of the sport would be more precious than success. So it is with the life-game upon which you are to enter. You know its ideals. You have said that they are yours. You will be as good as your word, and as proud as your heritage.

Some of you may have read the charming and stirring address that was given by Mr. Barrie not long ago as Rector of St. Andrews. He called it "Courage": and the courage that he praised and the courage that he invoked was the courage of the sportsman, of the young sportsman, the courage of adventurous youth. You will need it now and again in the years that are ahead of you. The tests of character come to us silently, unawares, by slow and inaudible approaches. We hardly know that they are there, till lo! the hour has struck, and the choice has been made, well or ill, but whether well or ill, a choice. The heroic hours of life do not announce their presence by drum and trumpet, challenging us to be true to ourselves by appeals to the martial spirit that keeps the blood at heat. Some little, unassuming, unobtrusive choice presents itself before us slyly and craftily, glib and insinuating, in the modest garb of innocence. To yield to its blandishments is so easy. The wrong, it seems, is venial. Only hyper-sensitiveness, we assure ourselves, would call it a wrong at all. These are the moments when you will need to remember the game that you are playing. Then it is that you will be summoned to show the courage of adventurous youth. There are some unquenchable spirits who never lose it, though the calendar may say that they have left youth behind and reached manhood or old age. "Be inspired with the belief," said Gladstone, "that life is a great and noble calling; not a mean and grovelling thing that we are to shuffle through as we can, but an elevated and lofty destiny."

You think I ask too much of you. I ask of you nothing that you are not competent to give. More than that, I ask of you nothing that will not mean success and honor if only you have the will and the strength to give it. I take as my text two utterances that have consoled and inspired me in many a doubting hour. The one is that of William James; the other is that of Emerson. The one shall stimulate your minds. The other shall cheer your souls. The one shall teach that intellectual effort is not wasted and never can be. The other shall teach that spiritual effort, the force of fine and noble character, is destined to a kindred triumph.

Skill is not won by chance. Growth is not the sport of circumstance. Skill comes by training; and training, persistent and unceasing, is transmuted into habit. The reaction is adjusted ever to the action. What goes out of us as effort comes back to us as character. The alchemy never fails. "Let no youth," says James, "have any anxiety about the upshot of his education whatever the line of it may be. If he keep faithfully busy each hour of the working day, he may safely leave the final result to itself. He can with perfect certainty count on waking up some fine morning to find himself one of the competent ones of his generation, in whatever pursuit he may have singled out.

Silently, between all the details of his business, the power of judging in all that class of matter will have built itself up with him as a possession that will never pass away. Young people should know this truth in advance. The ignorance of it has probably engendered more discouragement and faint-heartedness in youths embarking on arduous careers than all other causes put together."

I know not where you will find a more heartening or tonic gospel. Our fates are in our own hands. We make and remake our own selves. We are "the captains of our souls." Nature pants with the desire to make us what we wish to be. The wish is the reality. What we think, that we are.

So much for the triumph of mind and spirit in the shaping of our own lives. There is something even stranger. It is the power of mind and spirit to shape the lives of others. Here I hold fast to Emerson. Again Nature is inflexible, inflexible in beneficence for those who serve as she is inflexible in indifference for those who stand aloof. The words in which Emerson to the very end gave utterance to this faith are as fine, a wise critic has said, as anything in literature.

"If you love and serve men," he writes, "you cannot by any hiding or stratagem escape the remuneration. Secret retributions are always restoring the level, when disturbed, of the Divine justice. It is impossible to tilt the beam. All the tyrants and proprietors and monopolists of the world in vain set their shoulders to heave the bar. Settles forevermore the ponderous equator to its line, and man and mote, and star and sun, must range to it, or be pulverized by the recoil."

A robust doctrine this, and one for stout hearts and placid and unruffled souls. Not the less for that are its validity and power. There may be hours of discouragement and rebuff. When the course is run, we shall see them in their true perspective. We shall know in the end that the game was worth the effort.

"Most of the troubles of life," says the French philosopher, "would be avoided if men would only be content to sit still in their parlors." Ah! but they will not, even those of them who have the parlors, and that is their glory, if it is also their undoing. The ceaseless drive is there; the lure that prods and teases; the shining, if shifting, goal, which, like the lighthouses of today, may summon with a revolving light, but ever swings full circle, a beacon to the wandering traveler.

This is no life of cloistered ease to which you dedicate your powers. This is a life that touches your fellow men at every angle of their being, a life that you must live in the crowd, and yet apart from it, man of the world and philosopher by turns.

You will study the wisdom of the past, for in a wilderness of conflicting counsels, a trail has there been blazed.

You will study the life of mankind, for this is the life you must order, and, to order with wisdom, must know.

You will study the precepts of justice, for these are the truths that through you shall come to their hour of triumph.

Here is the high emprise, the fine endeavor, the splendid possibility of achievement, to which I summon vou and bid you welcome.

THE COMRADESHIP OF THE BAR[1]

Mr. Chairman, Brethren and Friends of New York University:

I HAVE no message for you today that is worthy of your greeting. I have come here as a friend to bear witness to my friendship. Your University has honored me with the guerdon of a degree. Your association, gracefully and graciously, has said that there shall be no distinction between sons of the whole blood and sons adopted of other parents, and in that spirit of fraternal fellowship has made me one of its vice-presidents. I have been brought within the family circle, and so I am going to talk things over with you in the desultory and intimate way appropriate for relatives and friends.

Perhaps I may say a word at the beginning to

[1] Address at a luncheon of the New York University Law School Alumni Association, December 20, 1927. Printed in the *New York University Law Review*, Vol. V, p. 1 ff.

those of you who are very young, the tyros of the bar who have the future all before you, and then another word that the tyros will share with those who are a little older, for as I look over this assembly I discover no one who is really old.

The fledglings of the profession are very close to my heart. In my days of practice at the bar, I used to act as counsel for a good many of the younger men, though, as I look back at it now, I can see that I was pretty young myself, and so I came in contact with my brethren, and with the most ingenuous, the warmest, the friendliest of my brethren, to a greater extent than many a lawyer whose experience in other ways was more extensive than my own. I was impressed in those days by the high quality of the work that could be done by youths of ability after a year or two of practice. The impression has been confirmed and deepened by my experience on the bench. I think the quality is due to the efficiency of the modern law school, which gives to the young men of the present a training that for breadth and intensiveness was utterly unknown to the law school of my day. The years bring their changes. In Lord Mansfield's day, a special box in the courtroom was set apart for students who picked their learning up by gathering such crumbs of knowledge as fell from their elders during the progress of the trial. There is a note by the reporter in one case that Mansfield requested one of the counsel to state the case for the benefit of the students in the box before the court delivered a reserved judgment. The noble lord believed, beyond a doubt, that he had been graciously condescending, and that his dutiful audience, advised of the dispute by this statement of the facts, would receive the considered judgment of the court with the meek and reverent acquiescence that was due to holy writ. Those were the good old days before law reviews existed, with the picked men of the law school as courts of ultimate appeal. The Mansfields of the present, if there are any, will know that they can get from students as good as they can give, at least if the goodness of the counsel can be measured by its vigor. I may seem to jest, but I am more in earnest than you think. I sometimes feel I might escape some of the mistakes that I am sure I often make, if I had the training that is given in the law schools of today. I went to Columbia Law School in the transition days when it was passing from the old method of instruction by textbook—itself a long advance over the method of Mansfield's time—to the case method now in vogue. I had been there more than a year under Dwight and Chase and their associates when Prof. Keener, fresh from Harvard, descended on a bewildered class. The course was so nearly over that he had little time to do more than endeavor to convince us that we had learned nothing in the past, were learning nothing in the present, and were not likely, unless we improved a good deal, to learn anything in the future, which truth he proceeded to expound with great variety of illustration, with much satisfaction to himself, and with effects upon the class varying from rage to incredulity, and from incredulity to despair. You have fallen upon happier days, the fledglings who have gone forth of recent years from the shelter of the law school nest. Whole fields of the law that have been traversed and explored by you were never opened to my gaze at all until I learned to know of them in practice. There was no course in corporations—none in constitutional law, unless one took an optional course in an allied school—none in international law, public or private—none in criminal law, except some optional lectures: and many other subjects that are now dealt with separately, such as bailments, carriers, bankruptcy—had only the incidental treatment that was given in a summary paragraph or section in Parsons' book on Contracts. You will wonder how we managed to worry along as passably as we did. They tell us of Lord Bacon that at the beginning of his career he determined not to practice. Lord Birkenhead commenting upon this choice, remarks that "a man of commanding and acknowledged intellect may well have shrunk from submitting with deference to the views of mental inferiors on the bench." I fear my self-revelation may have carried me too far, and may have filled you with disdain for at least one of the incumbents of high judicial office.

THE COMRADESHIP OF THE BAR

I had occasion some months ago to consider the statistics of application for admission to the bar. Until I read them, I sometimes thought that the popularity of the profession would wane with the waning importance of mere forensic skill. The throng of would-be lawyers is evidence that there was no substance to my fear. Yet a change there has been, a change even since my own time, and still more a change since the time of others who came before me. More and more the work of the lawyer is done in the office. The specialists in litigation are comparatively few. Many of my friends in the profession never go into court at all, and many more go there at infrequent intervals and with sounds of lamentation. Lord Bryce observed in his book on the American Commonwealth that the best intellect of the country was attracted to the bar. I feel quite certain that it is the court, and not the office, that is the attraction for ambitious youth. The struggle for justice would lose its zest if law could be turned, as I believe medicine is turning in some degree, into a prophylactic science ordered with such nicety that litigation would become as catastrophic as the plague. I feel sure that even now the dream of ambitious youth knocking at the door of the profession, is the dream of successful effort in the courts. New land-marks (they say to themselves) are to be raised along the ancient highways; new courses are to be marked where the lines of growth and development are still uncharted and uncertain; justice is to be made to prevail when threatened with defeat by its foes, the forces of deceit and darkness. Better still, the court is to be made to eat its own words or the words of its predecessors, avow itself in error, and right an ancient wrong. I do not mean to suggest that courts thrive upon such a diet, or partake of it when there is a fair excuse for choosing a dish less indigestible. All the greater is the thrill that comes to the implacable pursuer when the judge, driven at last to cover, reaches out for the cup of medicine, and drains it as befits a man. These are the dreams of youth, not always realized in life, but coloring, none the less, and irradiating the vision that lies ahead. If numbers tell the tale, the vision is still seen.

THE COMRADESHIP OF THE BAR

I have been talking to the fledglings. It is time to keep my promise and reserve some portion of my discourse for them and for their elders.

I was reading not long ago a series of addresses by Stanley Baldwin, Prime Minister of England. Delightful they are in their urbanity, their quiet humor, their mellow culture, their modesty and wisdom. In one of these addresses, he is talking to the members of his own party in the House of Commons. "Don't ever lose touch," he says, "with your constituency; don't ever mistake the voice of the clubman and the voice of the press man in London for the voice of the country. It is the country that has returned you; it is the country that will judge you." One would not give precisely that advice to a judge, and yet, in essence perhaps, the advice would not be greatly different. Let him not trouble himself overmuch about the voice of clubman or of press. Honest enough and well-meaning it will be, yet the artist, if he is to be judged with understanding, will throw himself upon his peers, upon those who are practiced in the art. So the judge, if he is to steer his course wisely, will never lose touch with the one constituency that is competent to judge him, the constituency of the bar. I count it a happy thing that the bar today has so many organs of expression by which it can make vocal thoughts and sentiments that might otherwise be uncommunicated and hidden. There are the law journals, increasing year by year alike in number and in power; there are the bar associations with their committees, their reports, their multiform activities; and now, with developing importance, there are the banquets and luncheons and receptions of these same associations, and of the graduates of law schools, where asperities of criticism will be steeped perhaps and mollified in the mellower and gentler medium of fellowship and friendship. All these organs of expression have a message for the judge who has the ear and will to listen. The law reviews will give him some hint of the unplumbed abysses of his ignorance. The bar associations by their committees will sum up his defects and merits with coldly critical judgment, and inform him whether the balance is plus or minus.

At reunions of this kind he will learn something else which has an importance almost equal. By these intimate contacts, he will be the better able to learn whether in the judgment of this high constituency he has permitted the official in him to swallow up the man.

There have been judges in the past who suffered that disaster. I am happy to report that the type is rapidly disappearing, if it be not quite extinct. I have something more in mind than the egotism that displays itself in harsh and overbearing manners, in explosive vigor of voice, or in a suspicious familiarity with the sections of the Civil Practice Act under the title of "Contempt." Exuberances such as these are at times the result of infirmities of temper not unknown altogether to the bench though happily uncommon; more often they are the defensive appliances of weakness or incapacity, conscious of its failings, and hopeful to divert attention by what seems to be a manifestation of its strength. I think there is another way, however, in which the official may submerge the man, more subtle, more insidious, if less odious and brutal. One can have an outlook on the law itself which will be the outlook of the drill-master rather than the genuine strategist, the official rather than the man. Take such a thing as the call of the calendar and the administration of calendar rules. There is a way of doing such things as a drill-master and a way of doing them as a man. I had little or no experience with such problems as a judge, so perhaps I have no right to talk of them—I have sometimes feared that I should make a mess of them myself—but, after all, I watched the doings of others while I was a member of the bar: so I am entitled to an opinion, whether it is worth much or little. Then when you pass from practice to higher problems, you get the same antithesis. Some of the worst decisions the courts have ever made have come from just this opposition. They thought they were not derogating from the soundness of a judgment when they admitted its brutality. I concede that there are times when the two will stand together—chiefly, I think, when the rule to be applied is one declared by statute. Yet the concurrence is rare, is to be viewed with deep distrust, and is to be deplored as much as it is distrusted. The common law, unless bound and riveted by statute, has instruments at hand of many varieties and shapes for the molding of that justice which is the end of her endeavor. The truth seems obvious enough, yet at times judges have been blind to it. Dean Pound in one of his papers tells us about judges who preferred a "strong" decision. By this they meant a decision that worked out some harsh result by the undeviating application of the method of strict logic to the development of a precedent or a rule. They thought that in so doing they were vindicating the power and majesty of law. So, in a delightful article by Mr. Buckland, a sketch of Frederick W. Maitland, we are told of an English judge who was said to exult in a harsh judgment, and seemed to be friendly to injustice when the choice was nicely balanced. Perhaps to these illustrations I should add the western judge whose strictness was a subject of one of Lincoln's anecdotes. "He would hang a man for blowing his nose in the street, but he would quash the indictment if it failed to specify what hand he blew it with."

I am not saying that examples so horrible as these can be found among the many judges I have known in years of practice too long to be stated at a festive meeting. None the less, the slumbering beast is in us, and may be waked to life and fury if we feed him overmuch. The ravening official will seek to swallow up the man. I interpret the invitation to be with you today as an expression of your judgment that whatever mistakes I may have made—and I know that they have been more than I like to figure or remember—I have at least avoided this one, I have not allowed the official to swallow up the man. I don't mean that I am entitled to a great deal of credit for so modest an achievement. In a court where the tradition of courtesy and equity is so ingrained and inveterate as it is in the Court of Appeals, one would have to be a pretty hardened sort of sinner to be guilty of the particular form of wrongdoing that has its origin in the pride of office. But then, when you come to think of it, virtues are important in the inverse order to the credit that is due to those who cultivate and practice them. No one of us struts about with satisfaction for the self-restraint involved in refraining from the crime of homicide, yet if the importance of the virtue were the measure of the credit we should all be crowing and cawing with the pride of moral excellence. So I don't assume to pride myself on the very modest virtue of being merely a human being. Charles Francis Adams says in his autobiography that as he looked back through the mists of the years the predominant feeling was one of satisfaction that at least he had gone through life without making a conspicuous ass of himself. That, I may say in passing, is my own paean of jubilation at the end of each judicial year. I am thinking that I ought to add another verse, a verse of thanksgiving that I have been able to be a human being. That is a modest achievement, as I have said. Perhaps it is not wholly negligible. I think we are coming more and more to a knowledge of the truth which I have been emphasizing today, that officialdom, however it displays itself, is the husk and that what is precious is the man within.

So I thank you for the privilege of meeting you as your comrade in this intimate and delightful way. It has helped and stimulated me. Your kindness is so great that I shall never know if the experience was impressed with a different quality for you. In the luncheons that will follow during the years that are to come, there will be brought together, with the tie of this Association to bind them, judges and lawyers of all qualities and degrees, good ones and, perhaps by some rare fortuity, poor ones, high and low, the men who have been successful, and the men who are waiting for success, but to whom success will surely come if only they are firm and strong. May the spirit of comradeship that has been ours today, abide with them too, and with the profession that we love.